DATE DUE

FRAGMENTS FROM GREEK AND ROMAN ARCHITECTURE

THE CLASSICAL AMERICA SERIES IN ART AND ARCHITECTURE

HENRY HOPE REED AND H. STAFFORD BRYANT, JR., GENERAL EDITORS

The American Vignola by WILLIAM R. WARE

The Architecture of Humanism by GEOFFREY SCOTT

The Classic Point of View by KENYON COX

The Decoration of Houses by EDITH WHARTON AND OGDEN CODMAN, JR.

The Golden City by HENRY HOPE REED

Monumental Classic Architecture in Great Britain and Ireland
by A. E. RICHARDSON

Guide to the Decoration of the Library of Congress,
compiled by HERBERT SMALL

THE CLASSICAL AMERICA PERIODICAL

Classical America IV, edited by WILLIAM A. COLES
(published as a book in 1978)

Classical America is a society which encourages the classical tradition in the arts of the United States. Inquiries about the society should be sent to Classical America, in care of W. W. Norton & Company, Inc., 500 Fifth Avenue, New York, N.Y. 10110.

FRAGMENTS FROM GREEK AND ROMAN ARCHITECTURE

The Classical America Edition of Hector d'Espouy's Plates

INTRODUCTORY NOTES BY

JOHN BLATTEAU

AND

CHRISTIANE SEARS

W · W · NORTON & COMPANY

NEW YORK · LONDON

Copyright © 1981 by Classical America
Published simultaneously in Canada by George J. McLeod Limited, Toronto.
Printed in the United States of America

Library of Congress Cataloging in Publication Data

Espouy, Hector d', 1854–1928.
  Fragments from Greek and Roman architecture.

  (The Classical America series in art and
architecture)
  Translation of Fragments d'architecture antique.
  1. Architecture, Classical. 2. Architectural
drawing—France. 3. Architecture—Details.
I. Blatteau, John W. II. Sears, Christiane.
III. Title. IV. Series: Classical America series
in art and architecture.
NA261.E613 1981   722'.8   81–430
ISBN 0–393–01427–4
        ISBN 0–393–00052–4 (pbk.)

W. W. Norton & Company, Inc. 500 Fifth Avenue, New York, N.Y. 10110
W. W. Norton & Company Ltd. 25 New Street Square, London EC4A 3NT

1 2 3 4 5 6 7 8 9 0

Contents

Acknowledgment

THIS publication was made possible by a grant from the Arthur Ross Foundation. It is the Foundation's purpose to renew and stimulate once again interest in Greek and Roman ornament and to further its application in contemporary life. Hector d'Espouy's objectives and the extraordinary quality of the wash drawings of the Prix de Rome winners inspired the selection of his book for sponsorship.

Hector d'Espouy's Plates as a Guide for Architects and Designers

JOHN BLATTEAU

I assert that he who has not known the works of the ancients has lived without knowing what beauty is.

—Hegel

TODAY, after a hiatus of fifty years, ornament is once again recognized as essential to architecture. In fact, construction without ornament may be described as mere building.

Ornament lies at the heart of the classical tradition, a common bond linking all great ages of Western architecture down to the American Renaissance (1880–1930). Evolving in Greece and Rome, classical ornament has stamped every great artistic era of Western civilization. In each period the work of the Greeks and, especially, the Romans was adapted directly or reinterpreted. Yet no matter the variety achieved, and the variety is infinite, it all reaches back to the world of the Mediterranean.

The practice of drawing Greek and Roman ornament has a long history. Leon Battista Alberti studied and drew the buildings of ancient Rome as did many architects and nearly all the painters and sculptors from Raphael and Verrocchio down to the Fellows of the American Academy in Rome in the 1930s. And those painters who could not make the trip to Rome often drew from casts of Roman ornament as these were exhibited at museums and art schools. Of all the recordings of this ancient work the most rewarding, because of their uniformly high level of scholarship and beauty of presentation, have been those of the French. As Hector d'Espouy explains in his preface to the original edition of *Fragments from Greek and Roman Architecture*, published originally under the title *Fragments d'architecture antique* in two volumes and here translated into English for the first time, the illustrations shown here are the drawings made by the winners of the Grand Prix de Rome while at the Villa Medici, the seat of the Academy of France in Rome. An *envoi* was required of each prize winner who had to study subjects of ancient architecture during his first three years in Rome. The drawings were forwarded to Paris to be shown to the members of the Académie des Beaux Arts, one of the constituent bodies of the Institut de France, which was responsible for the Rome Academy. After his first three years of study each Rome prize winner was free to take on more ambitious projects. The selection of the drawings published here shows the foundation that each Grand Prix man was laying, not only for his subsequent work in Rome but also for his future architectural commissions.

Although drawings of ancient ornament had been made for generations before the winners of the Grand Prix de Rome descended on the Villa Medici, the young Frenchmen were the first to go about the work systematically. The drawings were limited to, and solidly based on, the carefully studied remains. Further, their presentation in formal academic renderings offers more information than could possibly be supplied even by a large number of photographs. The key to the usefulness and success of the drawings is the adoption of an academic convention of representation. Light is always presumed to come from the upper left to the lower right at an angle of 45 degrees. This allows each object to be read in three dimensions, as the depth of the shadow is equal to the measurement of the projection of the object. Also, within the convention, an elaborate system of values was developed to indicate the relative distance between planes. When details are presented in this way we can not only see the objects in three dimensions but we can also compare one element with another for effects of scale.

Appreciation of the drawings in d'Espouy's *Fragments* cannot be complete without some explanation of the technique of India ink wash rendering. Extreme discipline is required to produce these finely studied works of art. Even the simplest drawings require painstaking care and preparation before any of the washes are applied. Great skill is needed to do the necessary linework. All of the information must be recorded before tone is even thought about. The drawing is then meticulously transferred in ink to the watercolor paper and the paper mounted on a board. The rendering itself requires infinite care and patience. Each tone is built up through many faint layers of wash so that the ink seems to be in the paper rather than on it. Each surface is graded so that the final effect of the drawing is that of an object in light and space, with a sense of atmosphere surrounding it. I cannot imagine the architect who has not looked with wonder and envy at these drawings.

The composition of each plate, as well as its technique, is worthy of study. There are line drawings of extreme simplicity, such as those by d'Espouy in his restoration of the Temple of Mars the Avenger in Rome (Plate A). His presentation of the Corinthian capital, with an elevation juxtaposed to its section and plans at different levels, makes the structure of this complicated architectural element clear to all. A great variety of the Orders are represented in elegantly rendered form. Edmond Paulin in his restoration of the Theater of Marcellus in Rome (Plate B) presents both the Doric and Ionic Orders with great depth and subtlety. The most elaborate compositions are those plates presented in the form called the "analytique." The term derives from the analytique or "order" problem, the first problem given to architecture students under the Beaux Arts educational system. It has come to stand for a type of drawing with a complex composition, one in which many elements of a design or

SECTION SVR L'AXE DV FLEVRON

PROJECTION VERTICALE DE FACE

DESSINS AV QVART DE L'EXECVTION

A. Corinthian capital and entablature restored: Temple of Mars the Avenger at Rome. REN-DERING BY HECTOR D'ESPOUY.

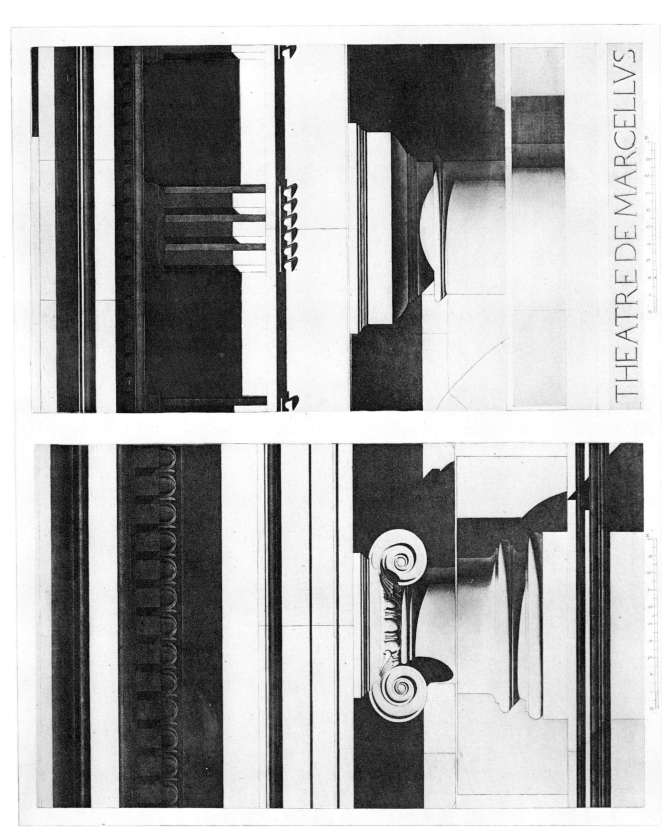

B. Details of the capital and entablature restored: Temple of Marcellus in Rome.
RENDERING BY EDMOND PAULIN.

C. Elevation restored: Temple of Hercules at Cori. RENDERING BY VICTOR BLAVETTE.

D. Various fragments restored: Basilica Emilia in Rome. RENDERING BY LOUIS-JEAN HULOT.

building are presented together, at different scales and in unusual combination. Blavette's restoration of the Temple of Hercules at Cori (Plate C) is a stunning example of this type of composition. Within the drawing can be found the temple elevation, its plan, and many of its details of ornament all beautifully arranged.

What, it might be asked, had the Grand Prix men to gain in making these very beautiful drawings? They already knew how to draw long before they went to Rome. They were learning to be architects by training their eyes in the use of proportion and in the distribution of light and shade.

They were also producing drawings which are works of art in their own right, and in no small measure this accounts for the fact that so many of these drawings exist today to be rediscovered. Altogether they make an unrivaled corpus of ornament to be used and adapted by the architect and the artist. They serve as inspiration as they show what can be achieved. They serve as models, directly or indirectly. As classical ornament can be made use of again and again, the examples of Greek and Roman work herein are always at hand for comparison and provide a standard by which to measure contemporary efforts. (See Plate D.)

We need only look around to see the influence that books like that of d'Espouy had on American architects prior to the coming of the Modern Movement. Ornament was carried throughout the United States as part of the classical tradition, from Independence Hall to the San Francisco City Hall. It was used prolifically in the American Renaissance where it was part and parcel of railroad stations, skyscrapers, banks, high schools, even early gasoline stations. It is interesting to note that the particular strength of the architecture of the American Renaissance in comparison with the work produced in other countries during the same decades was the American fidelity to classical models. Architects of the American Renaissance were well aware of the dangers of invention and of originality for its own sake, knowing that their inventions would eventually be measured against the models of classical perfection.

The public must involve themselves in questions of value and judgment in architectural design. So long as the public remains ignorant of the importance of ornament, architects can and will continue to freely indulge in fashion. Aided by these drawings of d'Espouy and by seeing the best examples of classical ornament, a knowledgeable public will be better able to influence architecture.

This edition of Hector d'Espouy's *Fragments of Greek and Roman Architecture* is visually the most exciting in the Classical America Series in Art and Architecture to date. It is an essential instrument for anyone interested in the future of the classical tradition in American Art.

Philadelphia 1980

Notes on the Life of Hector d'Espouy

by
CHRISTIANE SEARS

H ECTOR D'ESPOUY was born on May 8, 1854, at Salles-sur-Adour (Hautes Pyrenées) in the old Kingdom of Navarre. His childhood was spent at Cazeres, a charming village near Toulouse where his father was *juge de paix* or local magistrate. As with many artists, talent revealed itself at an early age. When a boarder at the Jesuit schools of Montauban and Toulouse he drew incessantly. The work consisted of skillful copies of lithographs reproducing old masters, portraits of his parents copied from photographs, and similar efforts.

In those days France was caught up in the restoration of ancient monuments, which had been sparked by Prosper Mérimée and Viollet-le-Duc. We today are horrified by the extent of the damage done in the name of preservation, and with reason, but we who are part of an age which despises ornament are hardly in a position to sneer at a generation which, in stripping ancient buildings of ornament, at least often replaced it with more ornament.

The church of Cazeres was not spared. To execute the restoration, the men built a workshop near the d'Espouy house. The young Hector became fascinated with the work being done and spent all his free time watching the artist of the restoration team mixing his colors, making sketches, executing drawings, and painting. He was enraptured at seeing decorative panels and screens beings made for obscure village churches. One day, in a sudden burst of enthusiasm, he solemnly declared to his father that he wanted to be a painter, that he was determined to be one. As might be imagined, the senior d'Espouy frowned at the suggestion because, to him, a painter was no better than a street singer. However, M. d'Espouy, impressed by his son's determination, came to a decision. If Hector wanted to be an artist, very well. But if he was to be one, why not an architect? And it was decided then and there.

My thanks to the following for their assistance in gathering information about the life and career of Hector d'Espouy: Madame Claudine Billières d'Espouy and Philippe d'Espouy, both of Toulouse; M. Rabier of the Hostellerie du Chateau d'Artigny, the former home of François Coty near Montbazon; the staffs of the Bibliothèque Nationale, the Bibliothèque de l'Institut de France, the Archives Nationales, and the Bibliothèque de l'Ecole Nationale Supérieure des Beaux—Arts, and especially Mademoiselle Guibert of the Bibliothèque du Theatre National de la Comédie Française.

The young Hector entered the School of Fine Arts of Toulouse as soon as his secondary studies were done. Then to Paris, where he was welcomed in the atelier of Honoré Daumet, one of the three architecture ateliers of the École des Beaux Arts. Daumet assisted Louis Duc with the west extension of the Palais de Justice in Paris and he rebuilt the famous Chateau de Chantilly for the Duc d'Aumale.

D'Espouy did splendidly at the Beaux Arts. In 1884 he won the Premier Grand Prix de Rome, which entitled him to a three years' residence at the French Academy in Rome and one year's travel in a country with classical ruins. He traveled all over Italy drawing and sketching. He executed a reconstruction of the Basilica of Constantine in Rome, which won him praise and, on his return to Paris, a First Medal in the Salon of 1890. He sought his beloved Antiquity in a lengthy voyage through Egypt, Asia Minor, and Greece. "Those noble edifices still appear to me as the highest expression of common sense," he wrote home. "They are of a perfection, of an exquisite simplicity. The more I analyze them, the more I am lost in admiration." He returned from Greece with a study of the Acropolis and the Temple of Athena Nike.

E. Hector d'Espouy, ca. 1905. COURTESY PHILIPPE D'ESPOUY.

On his return to Paris, although trained as an architect, it was by virtue of his skill in doing murals and in decorating that he obtained commissions. He decorated the Museum of Decorative Arts and the hall of the local stock exchange in Nantes. He designed the asbestos curtain of the Comédie Française. In the Panthéon he did a fresco over the entrance. He decorated the watering establishment at Le Mont Dore in the Auvergne in a style inspired by Pompeii. In Brussels he was the decorator of the Museum of Central Africa; in Lille, that of the office of the newspaper, *Echo du Nord*. Honoré Daumet, his old master, and Ernest Sanson called on him to decorate the grand salon of the Palais Rose, as it was known. This magnificent mansion, which stood until 1969 on the Avenue Foch, was built for Boni de Castellane whose wife, Anna, was the youngest daughter of the railroad magnate Jay Gould. Her dowry paid for the palace. Conspicuous among his commissions was the decoration of the Chateau d'Artigny at Montbazon near Tours, which was the residence of François Coty, the perfumer.

He executed a mural for the oval dome over the stairwell of the James A. Burden residence at 7 East Ninety-first Street in New York. He obtained this commission through the building's architect, Whitney Warren, who also designed the Grand Central Terminal and the New York Yacht Club.

In 1895 Hector d'Espouy was named Professor of Ornamental Design at the École des Beaux Arts. In 1905 appeared his *Fragments d'architecture antique d'après les relevés et restaurations des anciens pensionnaires de l'Académie de France à Rome* of which *Fragments from Greek and Roman Architecture* is an edited version. In 1925 he published *Fragments d'architecture du moyen âge et de la renaissance*.

Perhaps the best person to evoke an accurate image of the man is his granddaughter. "The recollection of the few years spent near my grandfather," Madame Claudine Billières d'Espouy remembered, "is an inexhaustible source of joy and happiness for me. There was a kind of complicity between us. We, my parents and I, lived in Paris in the same building as my grandparents. The two apartments were on the same landing. Both had balconies overlooking the lovely Luxembourg gardens. The huge studio of my grandfather extended the already vast apartment and there was a constant coming and going of students, models and friends. Hector d'Espouy liked to work surrounded thus cheerfully. Gaiety and humor spread through the house. Physically he was straight and tall, robust, life-loving. Morally he was, above all, an idealist, passionately fond of art, warm, kind, courteous, generous, broad-minded, modest. A charmer and a poet.

"His faults? Sometimes, an outburst of anger, soon forgotten, and a hopeless absent-mindedness. He used to go out for long walks either in Paris or in the country, often with me, a little girl of five or six, and he regularly forgot dinner time.

"An amusing episode comes back to me. It was in Paris, where he used to paint late at night in his atelier. One evening, deep in his work, he completely forgot that he had been invited to dinner by Raymond Poincaré, then President of the Republic. Suddenly, it came back to him, and realizing how late it was, he slipped on his overcoat in a great rush and left hurriedly. At the Elysée, the Presidential Palace, the usher took his coat and my grandfather appeared in his paint-spotted overall on top

F. "The Arts and Sciences", portion of the oval mural on canvas by Hector d'Espouy at the top of the stairwell of the James A. Burden house at 7 East Ninety-first Street, New York City (Architects, Warren and Wetmore, 1902). This residence is now part of the Convent of the Sacred Heart. PHOTOGRAPH BY JOSEPH FARBER.

of his dinner jacket to the great amusement of the President and his guests. This incident made the evening."

It was a happy life and the d'Espouys entertained frequently both in Paris and at Cazeres. His closest associate and friend was his son, Jean, who worked for him. At the outbreak of war his son was called to the colors; he came through the four years of service without a scratch. But, two years later he died. Hector d'Espouy was stricken: a tall man, he now stooped—his vitality depleted. He died in January, 1929, at Cazeres, where he could enjoy the Virgilian landscape that he had loved so much and painted so often—the chain of the Pyrenees on the horizon.

Hector d'Espouy's Preface to *Fragments from Greek and Roman Architecture*

translated from the French by
HENRY HOPE REED

ARCHITECTS who have won the Grand Prix de Rome are required, in the first three years of residence in Italy, to send to Paris work based on the best fragments of ancient architecture.

The major lessons of these studies lie, of course, in their execution, but they often give their authors the opportunity to sustain and increase their reputation. The studies are shown every year at the École des Beaux Arts. A large public sees them, as do the critics, and they result in a report by the Académie des Beaux Arts [1] which is published in the *Journal officiel.*

Every year, after a sharp competition, the Institut singles out a young architect for residence in Rome. Obliged to stay four years in countries where ancient classical ruins abound, far from the press of business and free of the burdens of everyday life, this artist chooses an ancient fragment and dedicates several months to measuring it and restoring all its mutilated parts. Then he presents the restoration by means of drawing which best convey the character of the original.

One can imagine the great quantity of beautiful and precious drawings thus produced by the Academy of France in Rome, now two centuries old, still flourishing and still productive of great artists.[2]

Most of this work has remained unpublished, much of it dispersed, some of it even being sent out of the country. But unquestionably—and the question has never even been raised—these drawings form the most conscientious and most complete study, the most accurate documentation available on ancient architecture.

From this enormous production we have undertaken to select that which seemed

1. The following academies constitute the Institut: Académie Française, Académie des Inscriptions et Belles-Lettres, Académie des Sciences, Académie des Beaux-Arts, Académie des Sciences morales et politiques.
2. With the coming of Modern Art, the program gradually eroded until it was abolished in 1968. The Academy of France in Rome exists but it serves entirely different ends. *Pensionnaires* are selected on the basis of their school record and not by competition and they are not subjected to a rigid program. Nor does the section of architecture exist at the Ecole des Beaux Arts as it did in d'Espouy's day. It is now one of nine *unités pedagogiques* in the Paris Region, where architecture instruction is given.

most useful in the instruction and practice of art. . . . We hope that this large selection of drawings may offer more than a series of documents to be copied. May it, above all, contribute to the refinement of taste and to the inspiration of beautiful creations. Antiquity has always provided the great lessons in good judgment, good taste, standards, and harmony. All work which deviates from this divine instruction seems to be struck by disease. By means of Antiquity, on the other hand, art without weakening itself adapts to the changing needs of society and to the demands made by new industries. Antiquity's all-inclusive system, if we grasp it, will lead us to give form to great arches of iron as well as to precious metals, to easy elegance as well as to useful objects.

To make Antiquity known will always prove beneficial. We will have accomplished our task if we lead several sympathetic persons to a study of the monuments which so many generations have relentlessly tried to destroy but whose remains still show to us, across many centuries, a distant ray of eternal beauty.

The fragments we offer have come down to us in sufficiently good condition to be faithfully reproduced in all their parts. In order to show how the fragments functioned in a building, we have included ensembles, and that has taken us through the imposing restorations which the pensioners of the Villa Medici [3] sent back after their fourth year abroad. But, as with the fragments, the few ensembles which we have chosen belong almost entirely to monuments whose remains clearly reveal the original structure. . . .

To the distinguished masters, to all the artists who most graciously lent their drawings, to all those who have kindly helped us, we offer our most profound thanks.

HECTOR D'ESPOUY

3. The Villa Medici on the Pincian Hill is the seat of the Academy of France in Rome, the oldest of the foreign academies and institutes in Rome.

A Selection of Plates from d'Espouy's *Fragments from Greek and Roman Architecture*

THE original d'Espouy volumes—entirely in French, of course—are to be found in most major libraries of art and architecture.

A word about the term "restoration" as used in this book: in undertaking their restorations, the Rome prize winners were reconstructing, or attempting to recreate, the probable appearance of Greek and Roman ornament and building from all available examples.

List of Plates

THE ACROPOLIS

The Acropolis, from the West, restored by Marcel Lambert (1847–?) *Grand Prix de Rome, 1873*

FAÇADE OVEST
RESTAVRATION

1

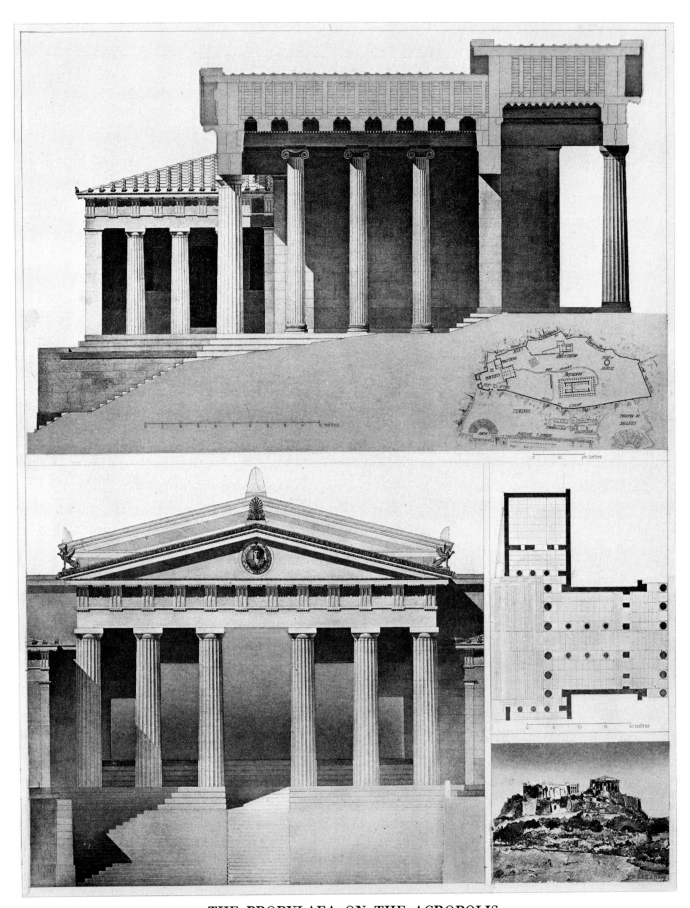

THE PROPYLAEA ON THE ACROPOLIS

General View and Longitudinal Section, restored by Emile Ulmann (1844–1902)

Grand Prix de Rome, 1871

ATHENES

PROPYLEES

DE L'ACROPOLE

ORDRE IONIQVE ET PLAFOND
DV VESTIBVLE

E. GUILLAUME

L. ULMANN

L. ULMANN

THE PROPYLAEA ON THE ACROPOLIS
Ionic Order and Ceiling, restored by Emile Guillaume (1826–1894) *Grand Prix de Rome, 1856;*
Ionic Column and Capital, restored by Emile Ulmann

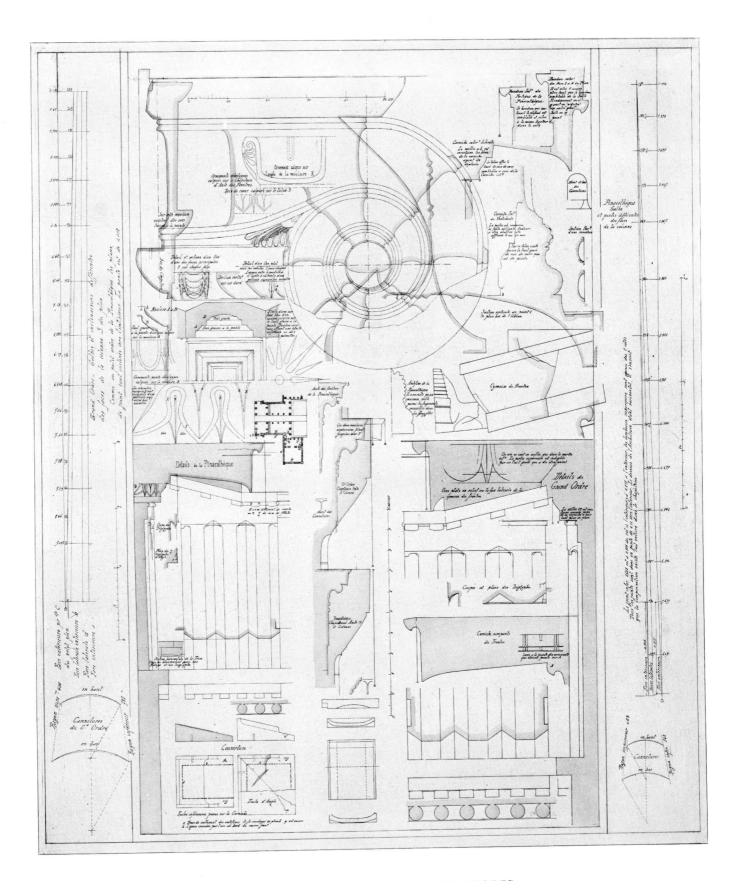

THE PROPYLAEA ON THE ACROPOLIS
Various details restored by Edmond Guillaume

THE TEMPLE OF ATHENA NIKE
Actual State and Restoration, by Honoré Daumet (1826–1911) *Grand Prix de Rome, 1855,* and Louis-Philippe Boitte (1830–1906) *Grand Prix de Rome, 1859*

THE TEMPLE OF ATHENA NIKE
Ionic Capital with Base and Entablature, restored by Honoré Daumet with sculptor
Henri Chapu (1833–1891) *Grand Prix de Rome, 1855*

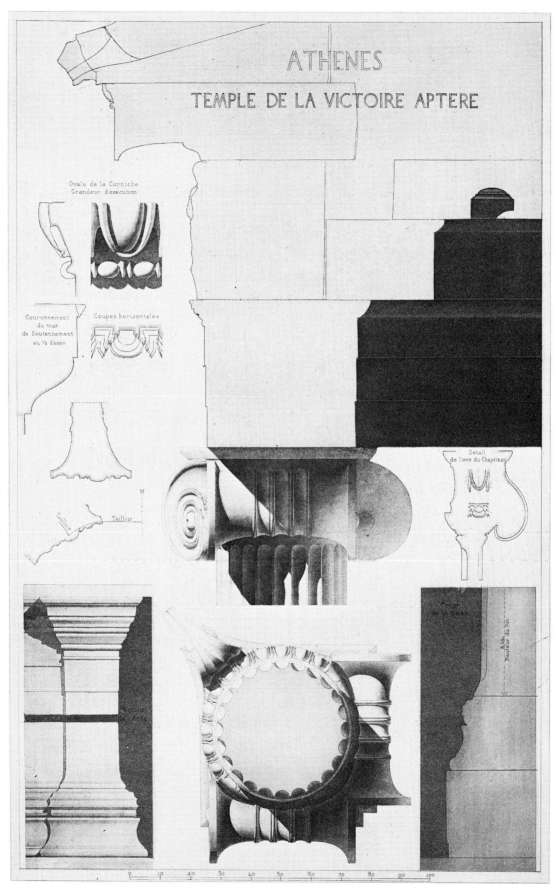

THE TEMPLE OF ATHENA NIKE
Ionic Capital, restored by Honoré Daumet

THE TEMPLE OF ATHENA NIKE
Ionic Capital, restored by Honoré Daumet

ERECHTHEUM ON THE ACROPOLIS
Ionic Capital and Entablature, restored by Léon Ginain (1825–1898)
Grand Prix de Rome, 1852

ERECHTHEUM ON THE ACROPOLIS
Entablature, restored by Léon Ginain

10

ERECHTHEUM ON THE ACROPOLIS
Ionic Capital and Base, restored by Léon Ginain

11

ERECHTHEUM ON THE ACROPOLIS

Actual condition and Restoration of the Caryatids by Emmanuel Brune (1836–1886) *Grand Prix de Rome, 1863,* and Léon Ginain

ERECHTHEUM ON THE ACROPOLIS
A Caryatid with Entablature, restored by Léon Ginain

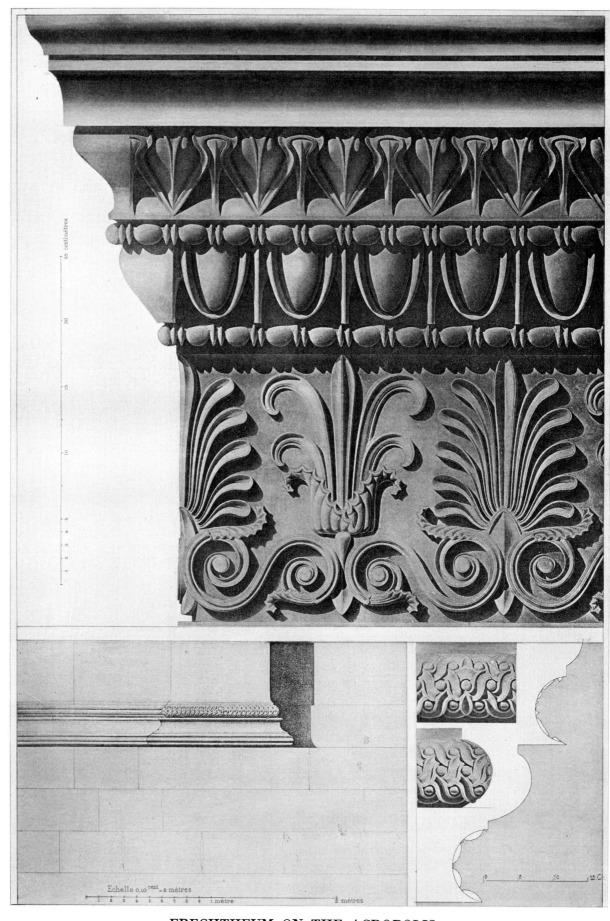

ERECHTHEUM ON THE ACROPOLIS
Details of Pilaster by Marcel Tétaz (1818–1865) *Grand Prix de Rome, 1844*

ERECHTHEUM ON THE ACROPOLIS
Details of Doorway by Léon Ginain

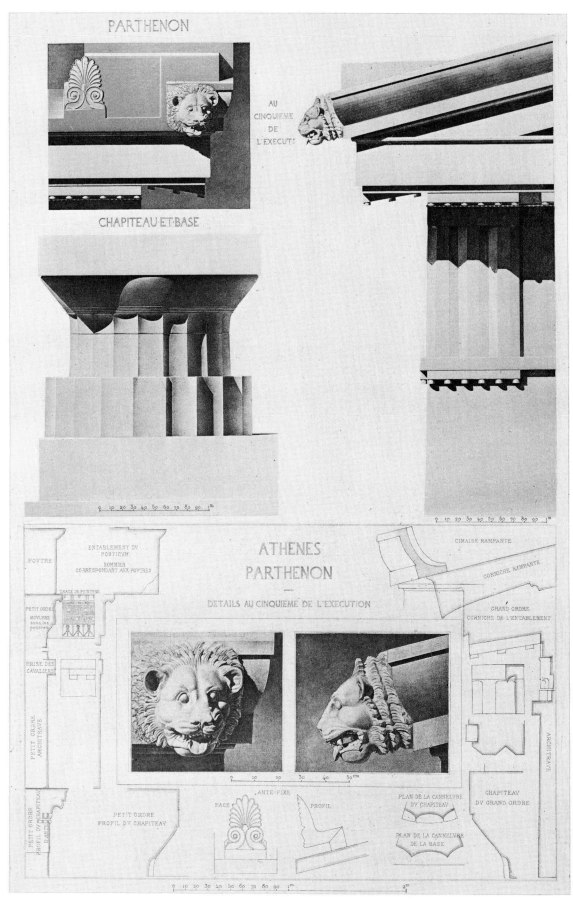

THE PARTHENON
Details, restored by Honoré Daumet

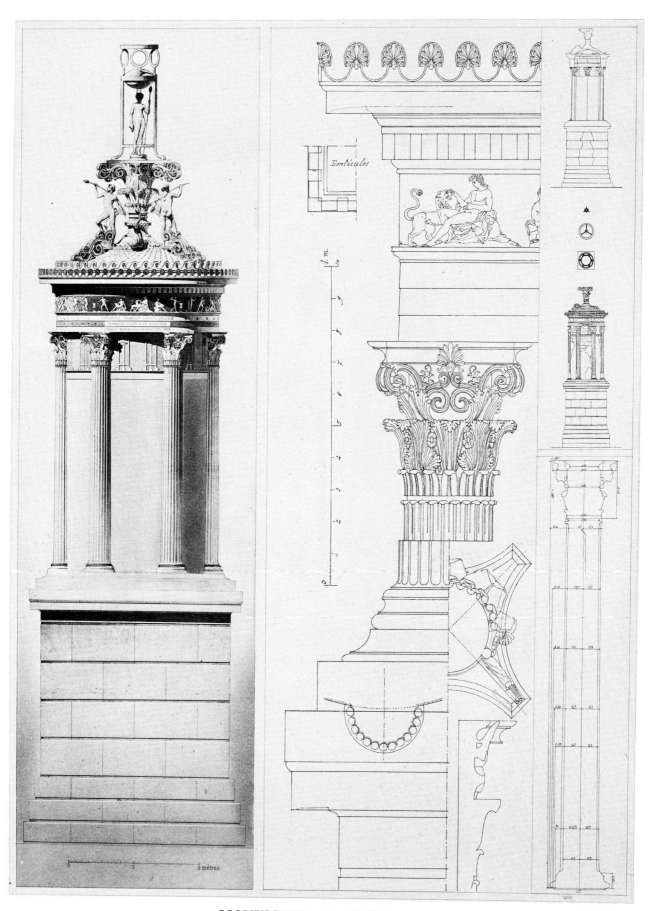

MONUMENT OF LYSICRATES
General View and Details by Edouard Loviot (1849–1904) *Grand Prix de Rome, 1874*

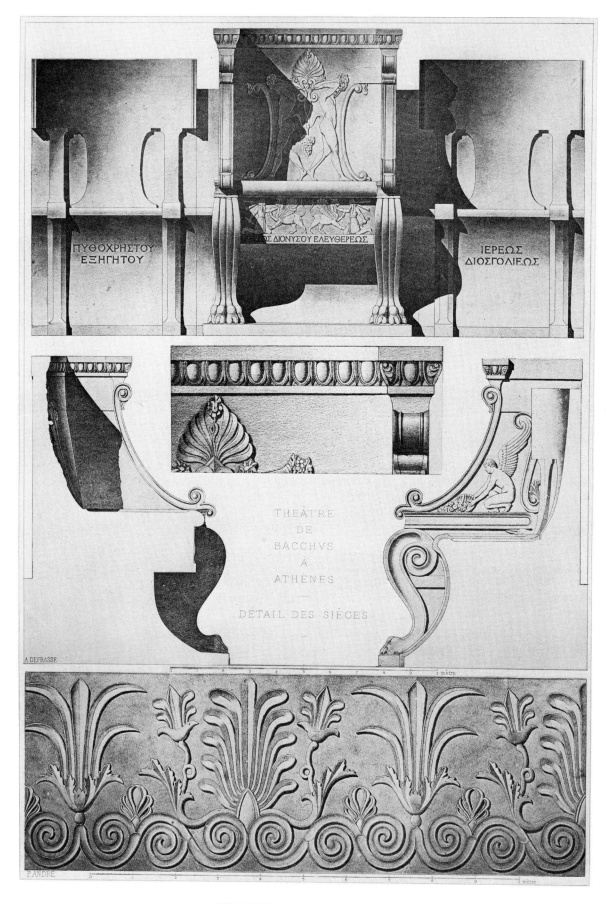

ΠΥΘΟΧΡΗΣΤΟΥ
ΕΞΗΓΗΤΟΥ

Σ ΔΙΟΝΥΣΟΥ ΕΛΕΥΘΕΡΕΩΣ

ΙΕΡΕΩΣ
ΔΙΟΣΓΟΛΙΕΩΣ

THÉÂTRE
DE
BACCHVS
À
ATHÈNES

DÉTAIL DES SIÈGES

A DEFRASSE

P ANDRÉ

FRAGMENTS IN ATHENS
Above, Throne of the Priest, Theater of Dionysus [Bacchus],
restored by Alphonse-Alexandre Defrasse (1860–1939) *Grand Prix de Rome, 1886,*
and Frieze from the Acropolis by Pierre André (1860–?) *Grand Prix de Rome, 1885*

POMPEII
Details of Triangular Forum and Various Fragments, restored by Ferdinand Dutert (1845–1906)
Grand Prix de Rome, 1869, and Auguste Ancelet (1829–1895) *Grand Prix de Rome, 1857*

POMPEII
Various Fragments by Edmond Paulin (1848–1915) *Grand Prix de Rome, 1875*

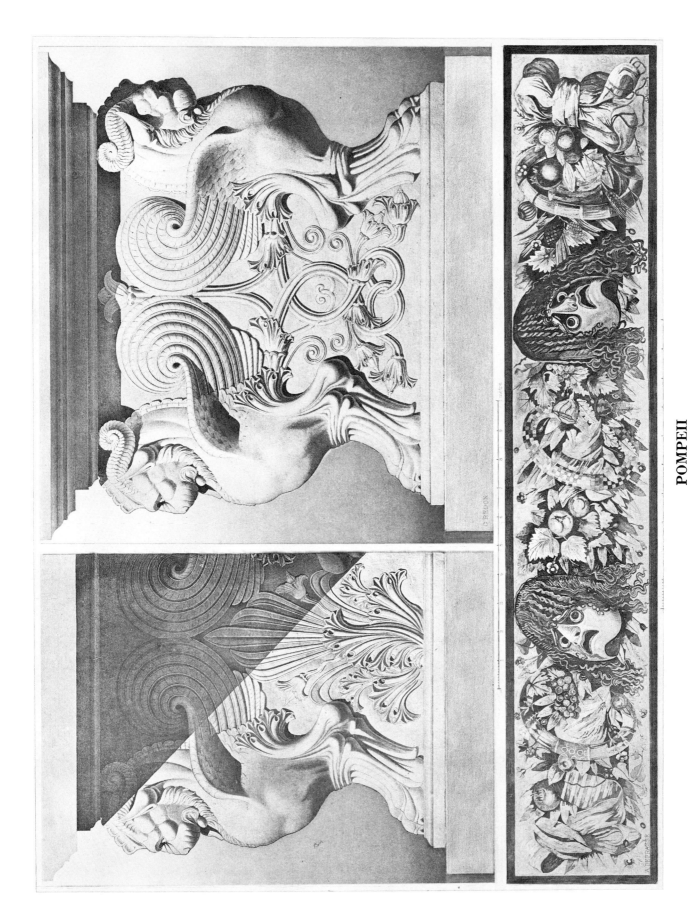

POMPEII

Left, Bench Support by Gaston Redon (1853–1921) *Grand Prix de Rome, 1883; right,* Mosaic by Alphonse-Alexandre Defrasse

POMPEII AND ROME

Above, Vase by Constant Moyaux (1835–1911) *Grand Prix de Rome, 1861,* and
below, Vase-Fountain, or, Rhyton, found in 1875 on the Esquiline near the site of the
Villa Caetani, restored by Hector d'Espouy (1854–1929) *Grand Prix de Rome, 1884*

22

DESSOVS DE VASQVE · MVSÉE DV CAPITOLE · RESTAVRATION
CHAPITEAVX ET PILASTRES · MVSÉE DE LATRAN · B: RELIEFS · VILLA ALBANI · ROME 1887

PATTERNS FOUND IN ROME
Various Fragments, found on the Esquiline near the Piazza Dante and now in the
Palace of the Conservatori, by Hector d'Espouy

23

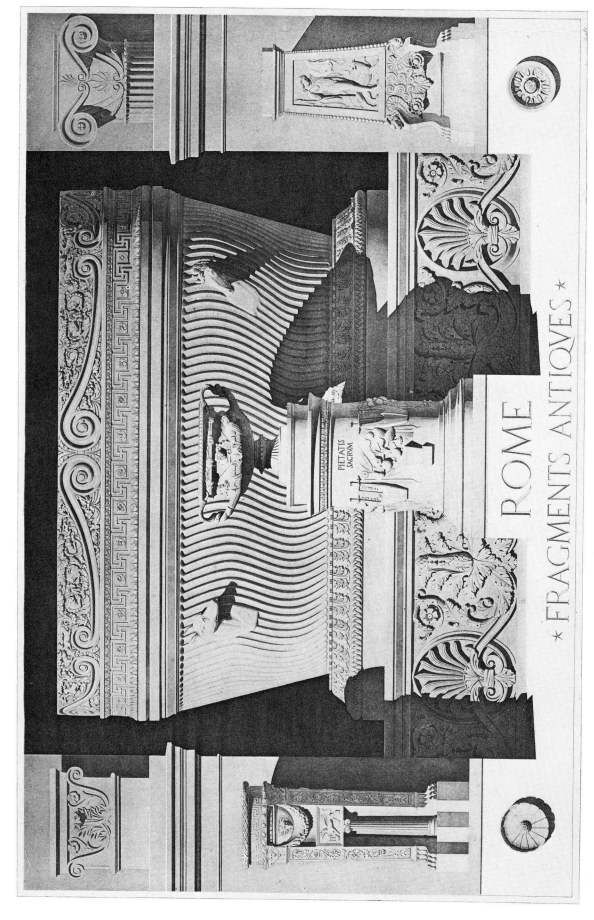

PATTERNS FOUND IN ROME
Ancient Fragments by Auguste Ancelet

24

PATTERNS FOUND IN ROME
Ancient Fragments by Auguste Ancelet

TEMPLE OF HERCULES AT CORI

Elevation, restored by Victor Blavette (1850–?) *Grand Prix de Rome, 1879*

26

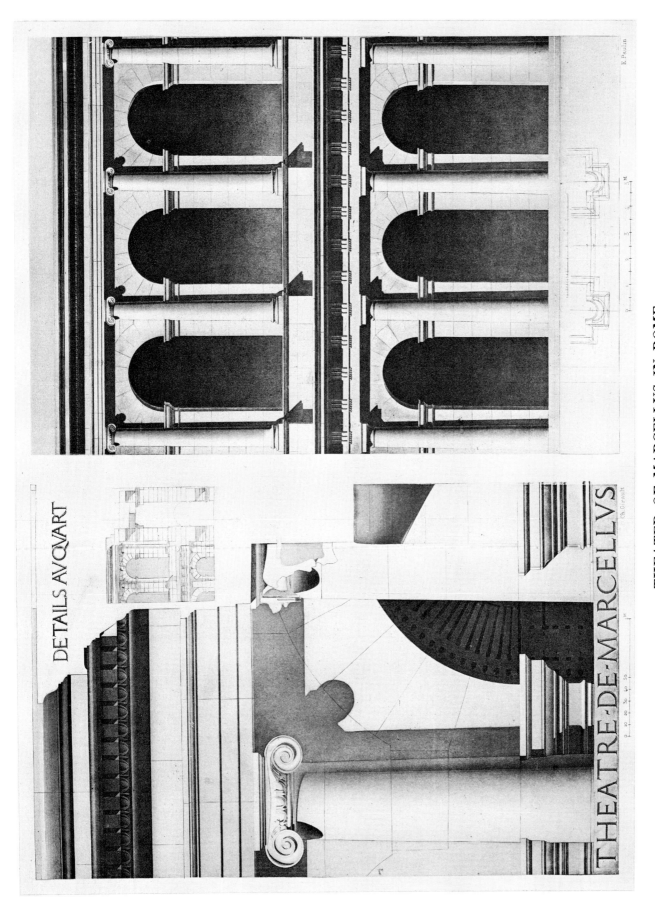

THEATER OF MARCELLUS IN ROME

Left, Details, restored by Charles Girault (1851–1932) *Grand Prix de Rome, 1880;*
right, Elevations, restored by Edmond Paulin

27

THEATER OF MARCELLUS IN ROME
Details, restored by Edmond Guillaume

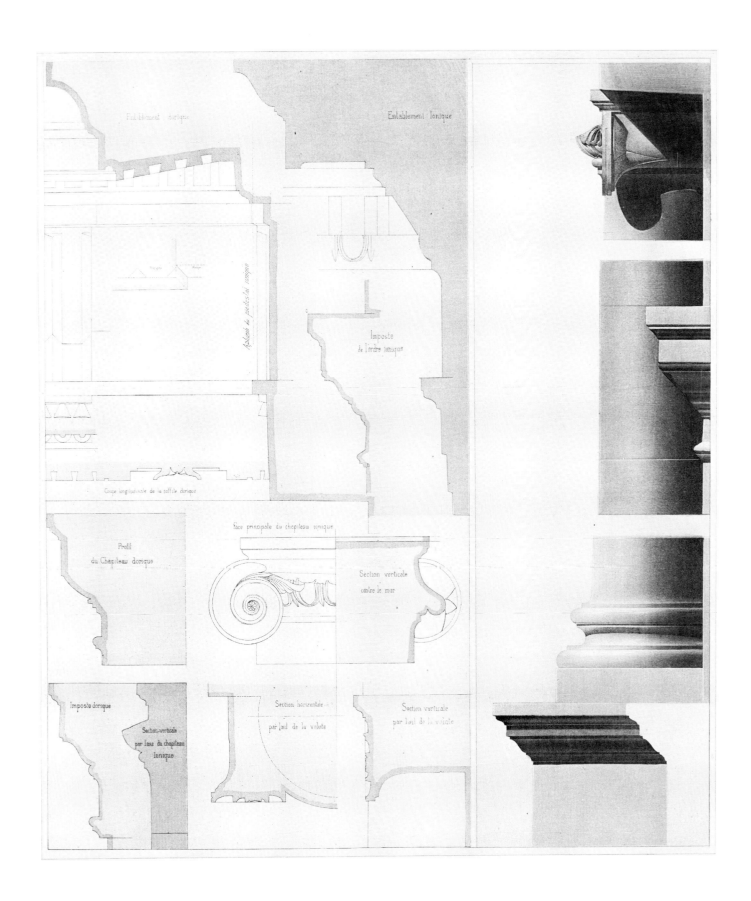

THEATER OF MARCELLUS IN ROME
Details, restored by Edmond Guillaume

29

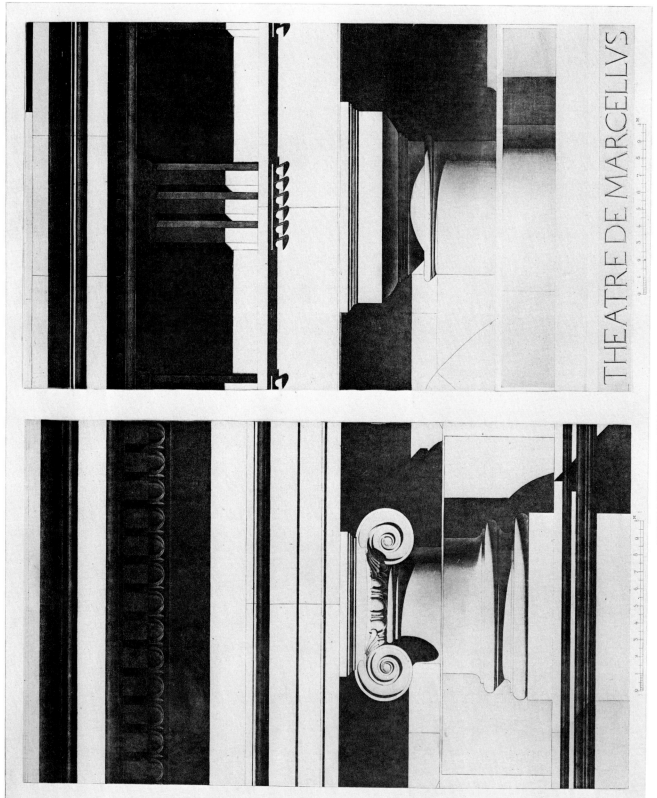

THEATRE DE MARCELLVS

THEATER OF MARCELLUS IN ROME
Details, restored by Edmond Paulin

SO-CALLED TEMPLE OF VESTA IN ROME
Plan, Elevations, and Columns, restored by Charles Garnier (1825–1898) *Grand Prix de Rome, 1848*

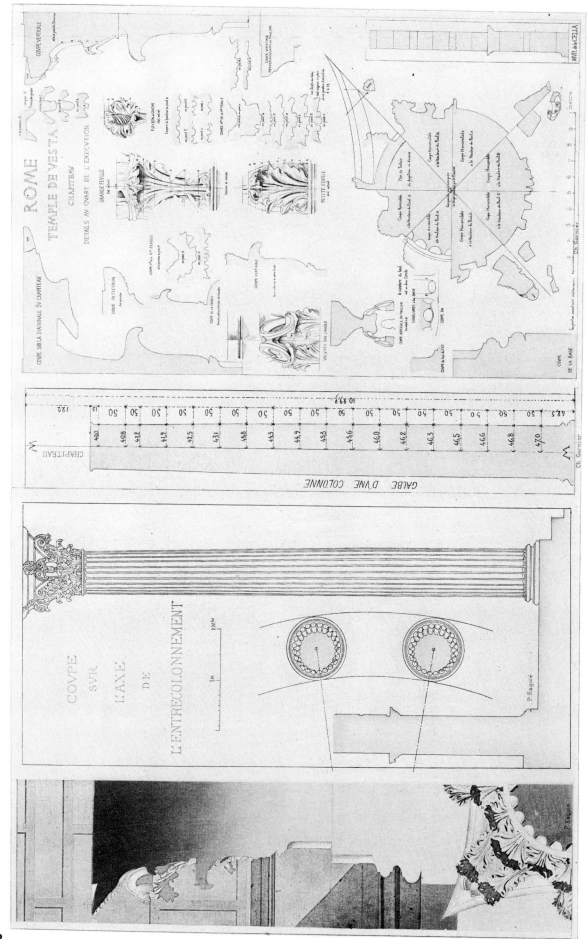

SO-CALLED TEMPLE OF VESTA IN ROME
Column and Details, restored by Charles Garnier and Pierre Esquié (1853–?) *Grand Prix de Rome, 1882*

SO-CALLED TEMPLE OF VESTA IN ROME
Capital, restored by Charles Garnier

33

SO-CALLED TEMPLE OF VESTA IN ROME
Capital, restored by Pierre Esquie

34

TEMPLE OF VESTA OR SYBIL AT TIVOLI
General View and Details, restored by Paul Nénot (1853–1934) *Grand Prix de Rome, 1877*

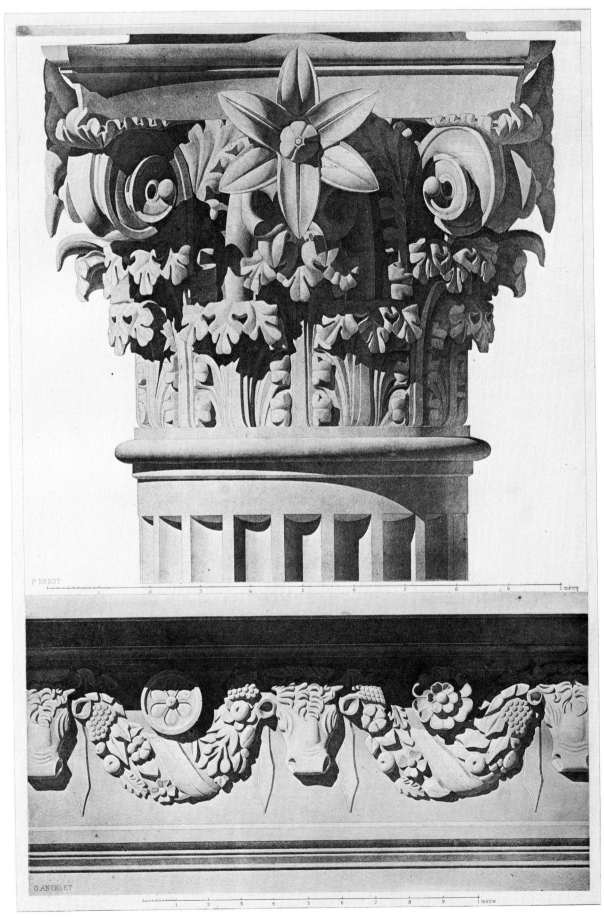

TEMPLE OF VESTA OR SYBIL AT TIVOLI

Above, Capital, restored by Paul Nénot; *below*, Entablature, restored by Auguste Ancelet

36

TEMPLE OF VESTA OR SYBIL AT TIVOLI
Various details, restored by Auguste Ancelet

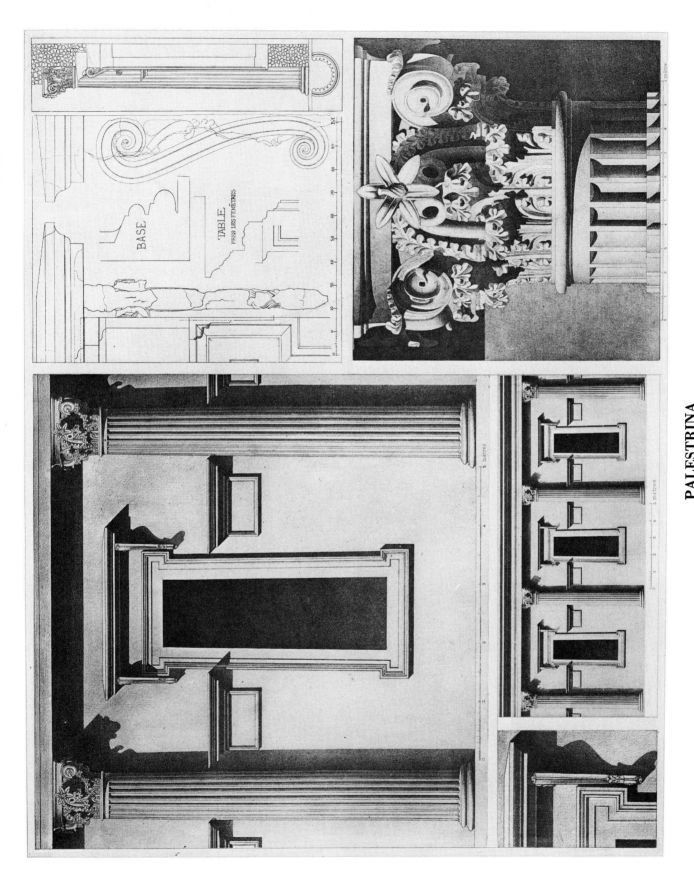

PALESTRINA
Fragments, restored by Louis Bernier (1845–1919) *Grand Prix de Rome, 1872*

DETAILS

SECTION D'VN CHAPITEAV

a 0.20 au dessus de l'astragale

BASE ET
PARTIE SVPERIEVRE
DVNE COLONNE

nom recouvertes de stuc

PROFIL

D'VN

PIEDESTAL

SECTION FAITE SVR L'ANGLE   PROFIL DV TAILLOIR

TEMPLE OF MINERVA AT ASSISI
Capitals and Bases, restored by Louis Bernier

39

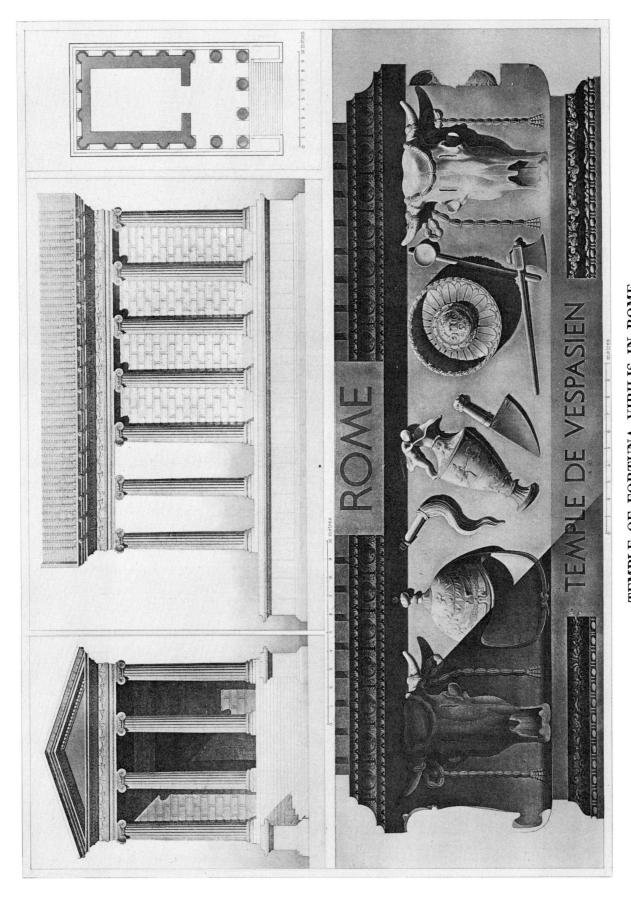

TEMPLE OF FORTUNA VIRILIS IN ROME

Above, General View, restored by Paul Blondel (1847–1897) *Grand Prix de Rome, 1881;*
TEMPLE OF VESPASIAN IN ROME Frieze, restored by Paul Blondel

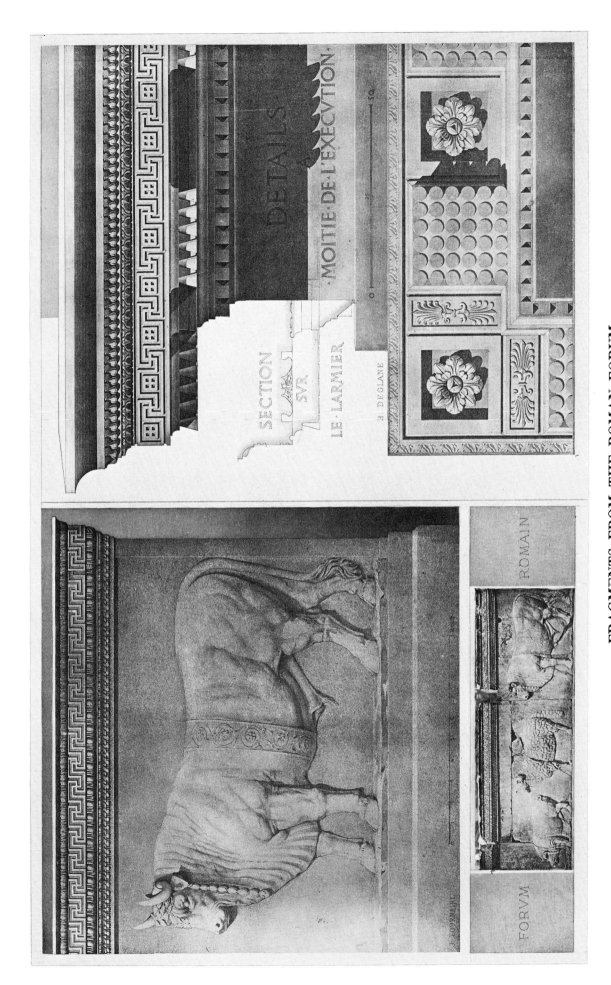

FRAGMENTS FROM THE ROMAN FORUM

Left, Other Fragments by Albert Tournaire (1862–1957) *Grand Prix de Rome, 1888; right,* Cornice, restored by Henri Deglane (1855–1931) *Grand Prix de Rome, 1881*

41

TEMPLE OF MARS ULTOR OR MARS THE AVENGER IN ROME
Elevations, restored by Julien Guadet (1834–1908) *Grand Prix de Rome, 1864*

TEMPLE OF MARS ULTOR OR MARS THE AVENGER IN ROME
Elevations, restored by Julien Guadet

43

TEMPLE OF MARS ULTOR OR MARS THE AVENGER IN ROME
Corinthian Capital and Frieze, restored by Ferdinand Dutert

TEMPLE OF MARS ULTOR OR MARS THE AVENGER IN ROME
Corinthian Capital, restored by Victor Blavette

TEMPLE OF MARS ULTOR OR MARS THE AVENGER IN ROME
Perspective of Corinthian Capital, restored by Hector d'Espouy

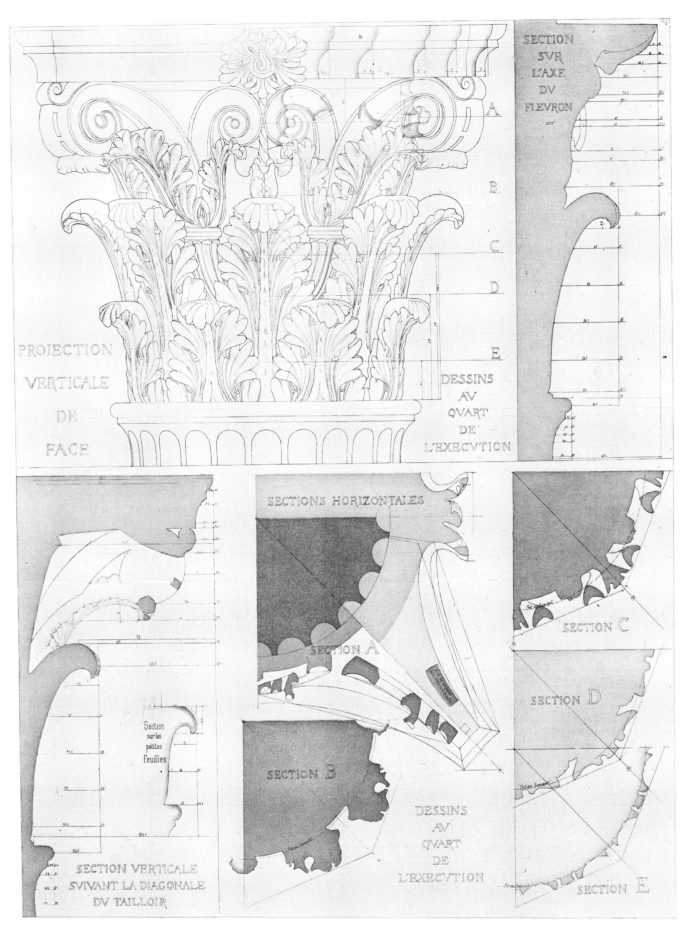

SECTION
SVR
L'AXE
DV
FLEVRON

A
B
C
D
E

PROJECTION
VERTICALE
DE
FACE

DESSINS
AV
QVART
DE
L'EXECVTION

SECTIONS HORIZONTALES

SECTION A

SECTION B

SECTION C

SECTION D

SECTION E

Section
sur les
petites
feuilles

SECTION VERTICALE
SVIVANT LA DIAGONALE
DV TAILLOIR

DESSINS
AV
QVART
DE
L'EXECVTION

TEMPLE OF MARS ULTOR OR MARS THE AVENGER IN ROME
Details of Corinthian Capital by Hector d'Espouy

47

TEMPLE OF MARS ULTOR OR MARS THE AVENGER IN ROME
Ceiling, restored by Victor Blavette

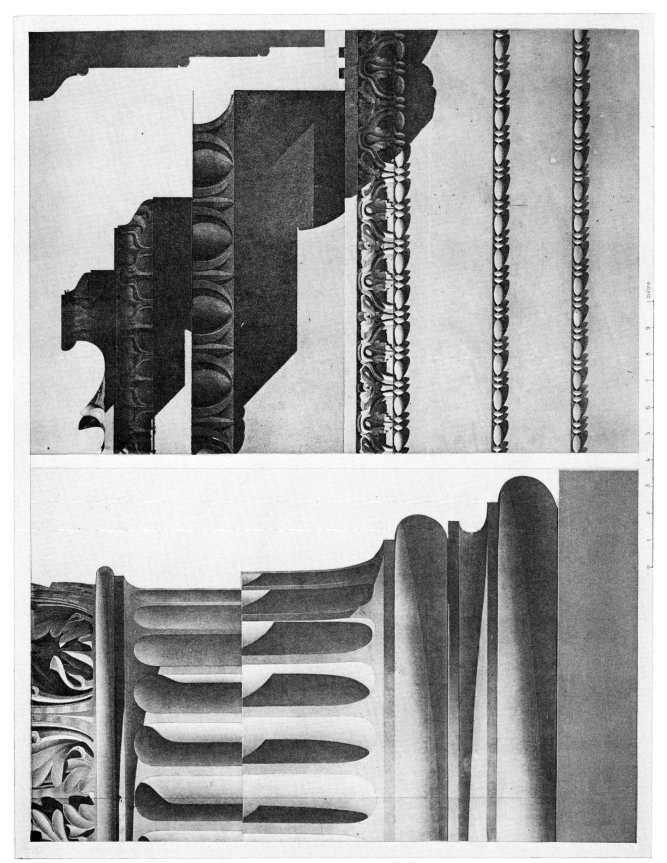

TEMPLE OF MARS ULTOR OR MARS THE AVENGER IN ROME
Details of Entablature, Base, and Fluting, restored by Victor Blavette

49

TEMPLE OF MARS ULTOR OR MARS THE AVENGER IN ROME
Details of the Coffering by Gaston Redon

TEMPLE OF MARS ULTOR OR MARS THE AVENGER IN ROME
Above, Interior Capital, restored by Henri Deglane; *below*, Vitruvian Scroll, restored by Léon Nénot

51

ENTABLEMENT
DV
TEMPLE DV SOLEIL
A
ROME

DETAIL AV QVART DE
L'EXECVTION

TEMPLE OF THE SUN IN ROME
Entablature, restored by Pierre Esquié

52

TEMPLE OF THE SUN IN ROME
Details of Entablature by Pierre Esquié

53

TEMPLE OF THE SUN IN ROME

Different Details of the Entablature (to be found in the Colonna Gardens) : Frieze, restored by Ferdinand Dutert; Cyma, restored by Pierre Esquié; Underside of frieze, restored by Julien Guadet

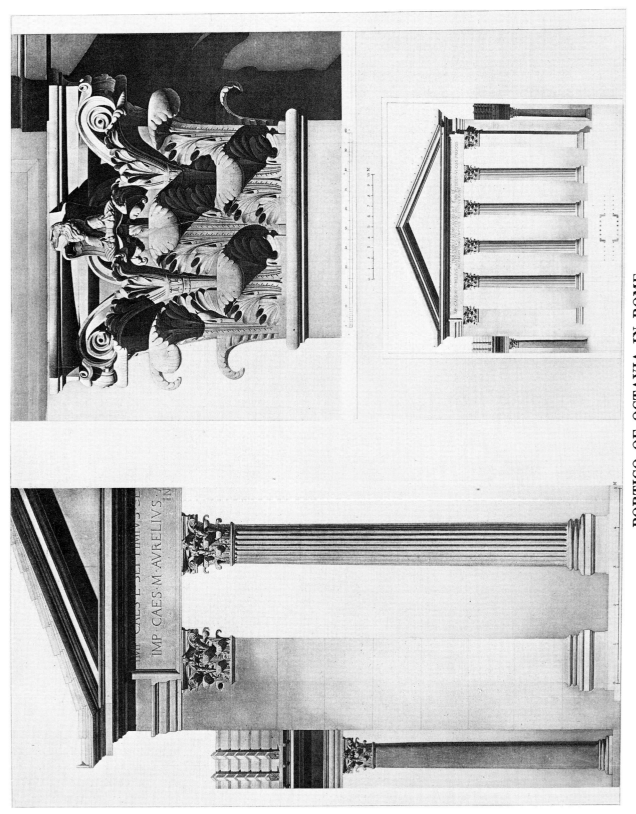

PORTICO OF OCTAVIA IN ROME

General View by Edmond Paulin (See plate 65 for the inscription on the Portico of Octavia by Edmond Paulin)

PORTICO OF OCTAVIA IN ROME
Details, restored by Edmond Paulin

TEMPLE OF ROME AND AUGUSTUS AT ANCYRA (ANKARA) IN TURKEY
Details of Door, restored by Edmond Guillaume

THE PANTHEON

General View and Plan by Felix Duban (1797–1870) *Grand Prix de Rome, 1823*

ENTABLEMENT
AU QUART DE L'EXÉCUTION

10 20 30 40 50 60 70 80 90 1M

THE PANTHEON
Corner of Pediment of Porch by Honoré Daumet

59

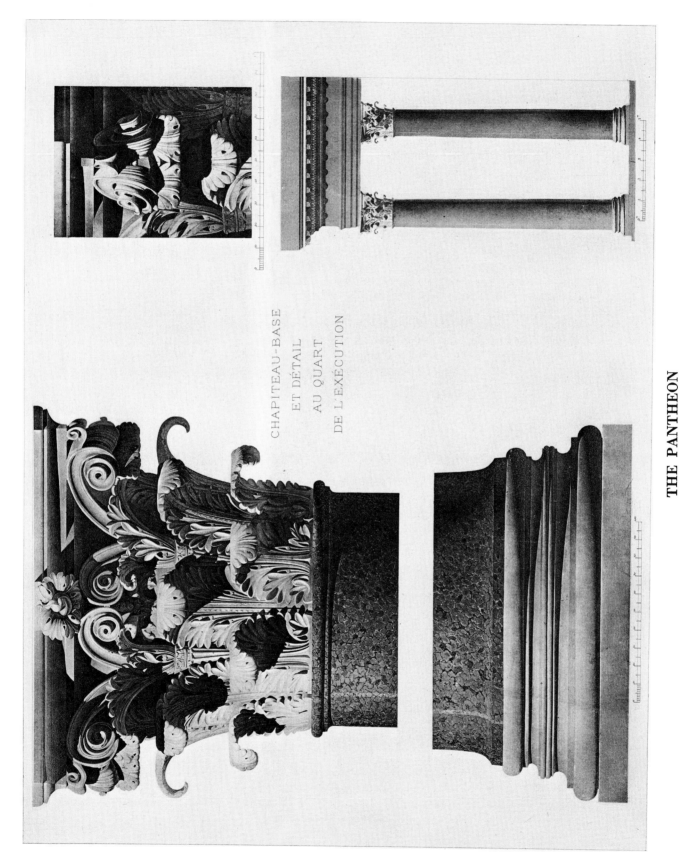

CHAPITEAU-BASE
ET DÉTAIL
AU QUART
DE L'EXÉCUTION

THE PANTHEON
Corinthian Capital and Base by Honoré Daumet

THE PANTHEON
Part of Corinthian Capital by Honoré Daumet

THE PANTHEON
Door, restored by Edmond Paulin

THE PANTHEON AND FORUM OF TRAJAN

Above, Garland near Door of the Pantheon, restored by Pierre Esquié, and *below*, Eagle and Wreath from the Forum of Trajan, restored by Pierre André (now found in the porch of the Church of the Santi Apostoli)

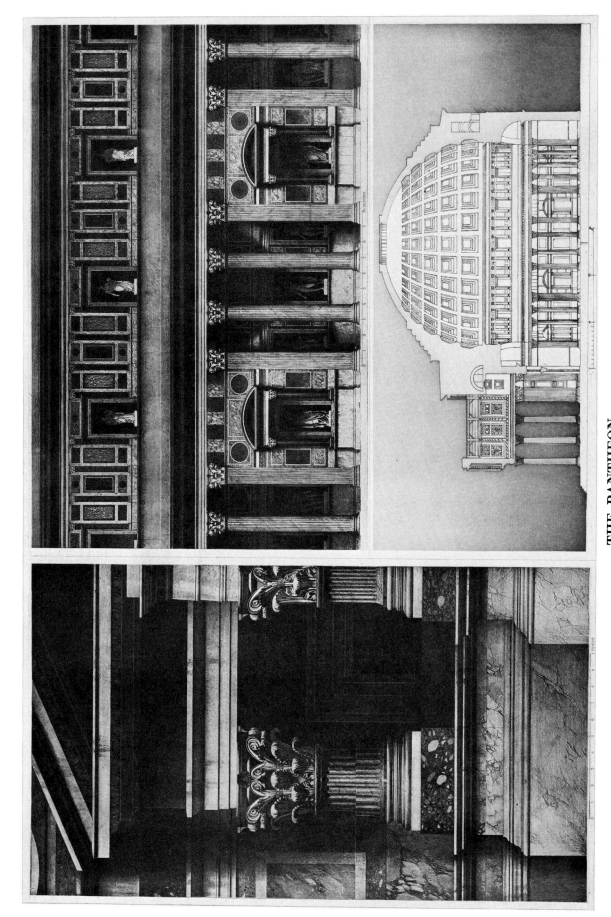

THE PANTHEON

General View and Details of the Interior, restored by Emmanuel Brune

64

THE PANTHEON AND PORTICO OF OCTAVIA

Fragments at the Back of the Pantheon, restored by Victor Blavette and Louis Sortais (1860–1911)
Grand Prix de Rome, 1890, and Inscription from the Portico of Octavia in Rome by Edmond Paulin

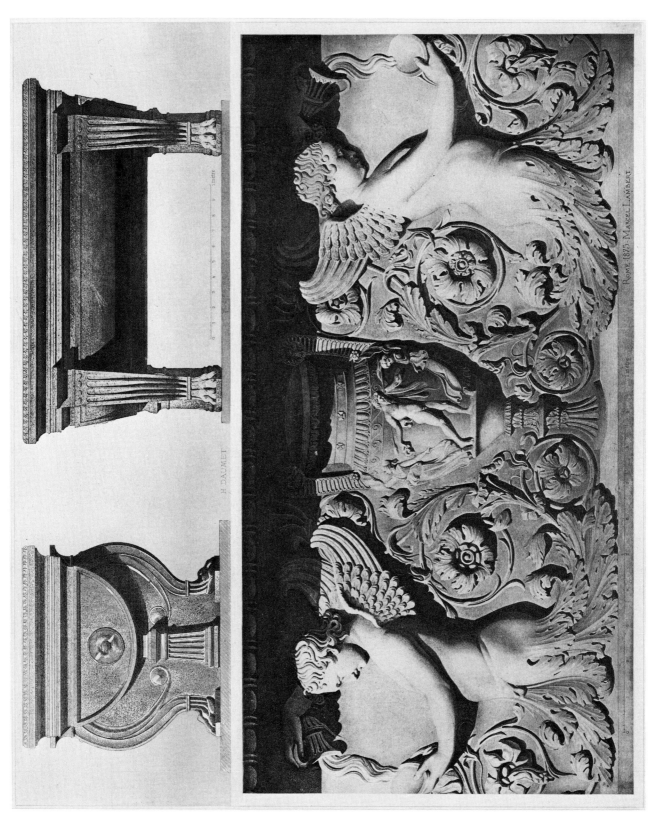

ROMAN PORPHYRY SARCOPHAGUS by Honoré Daumet
(Now in the Corsini Chapel in St. John Lateran, it formerly stood in the porch of the Pantheon.)
FORUM OF TRAJAN Fragment, restored by Marcel Lambert

66

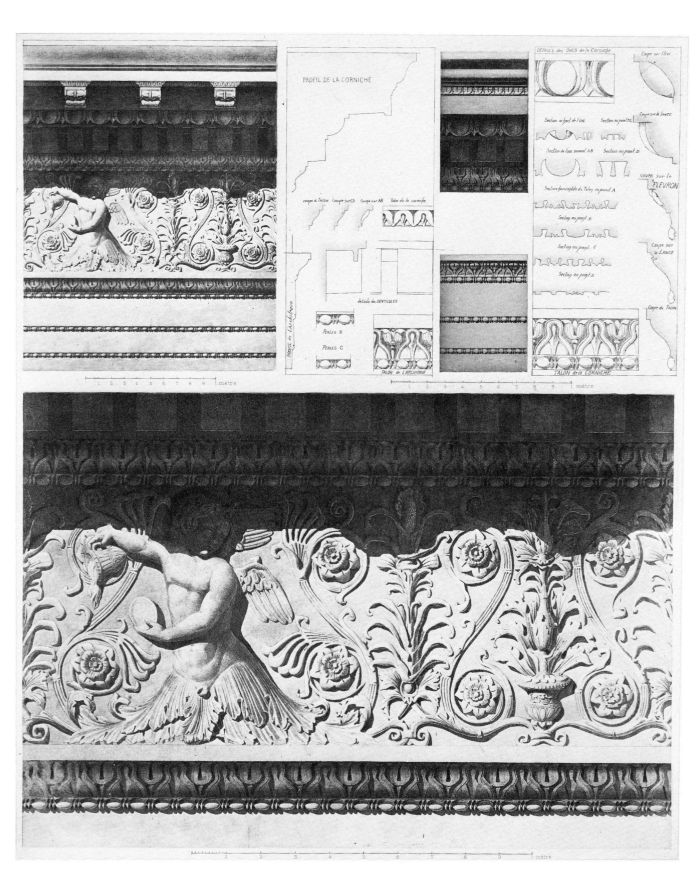

FORUM OF TRAJAN
Fragments, restored by Charles Garnier

ROME
—
BASILIQVE
·
VLPIENNE
—

MVSEE
DE
LATRAN

THE BASILICA ULPIA
Fragment, restored by Pierre André (Capitals shown at bottom of plate to be found in
the Lateran Museum)

COLUMN OF TRAJAN
Restoration by Léon Ginain

69

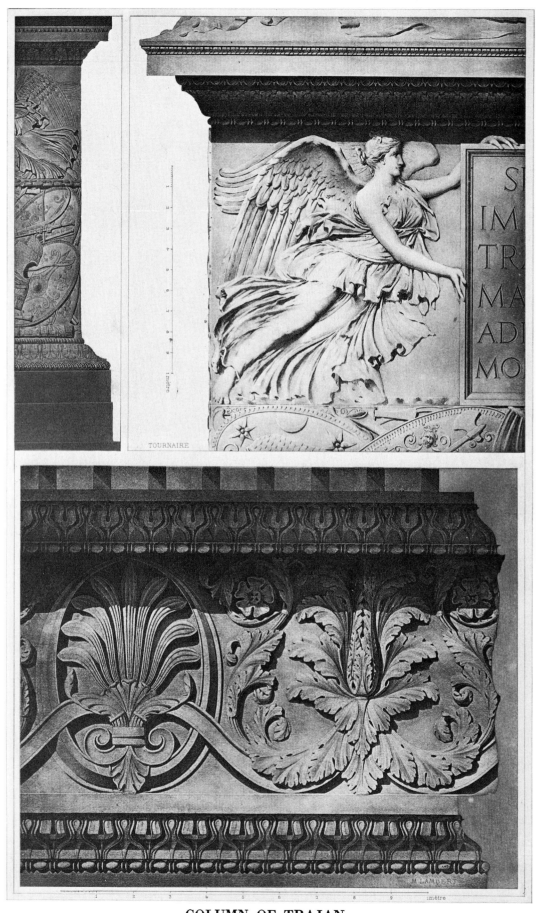

COLUMN OF TRAJAN
Above, Details, restored by Albert Tournaire; *below*, FORUM OF TRAJAN
Fragment from the Forum of Trajan, restored by Marcel Lambert

70

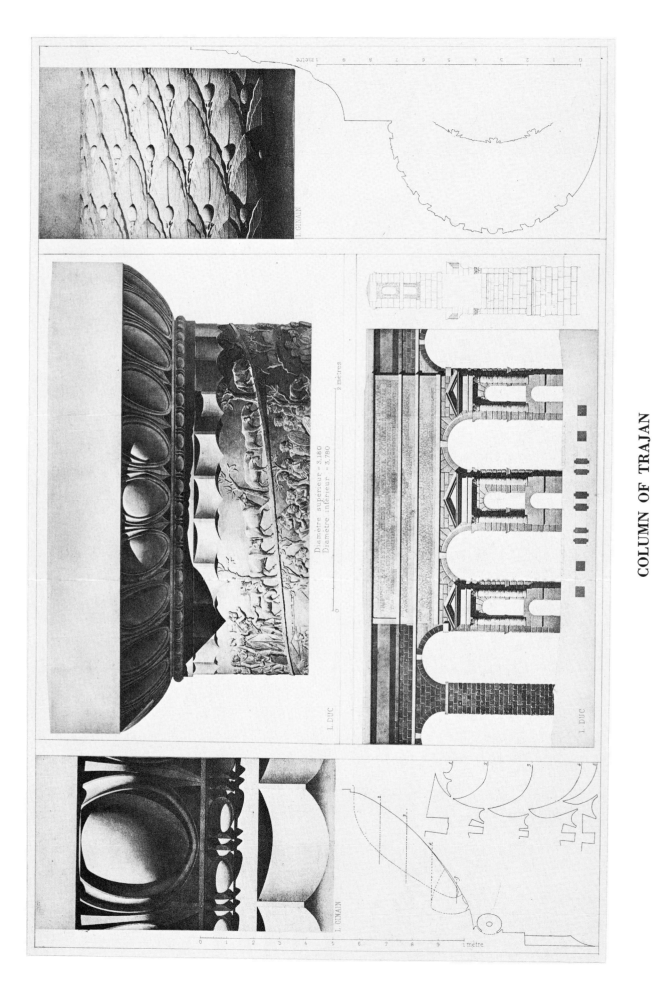

COLUMN OF TRAJAN

Above, Details of the Column, restored by Louis Duc (1802–1879) *Grand Prix de Rome,
1825*, and Léon Ginain; *below*, AQUEDUCT OF CLAUDIUS Restoration by Louis Duc

71

DIFFERENT FRAGMENTS

Left, Other Fragments Now at the Villa Medici, restored by Julien Guadet; *right,*
Decorative Pattern Now in the Court of the Fiano Palace in Rome, restored by Charles Girault

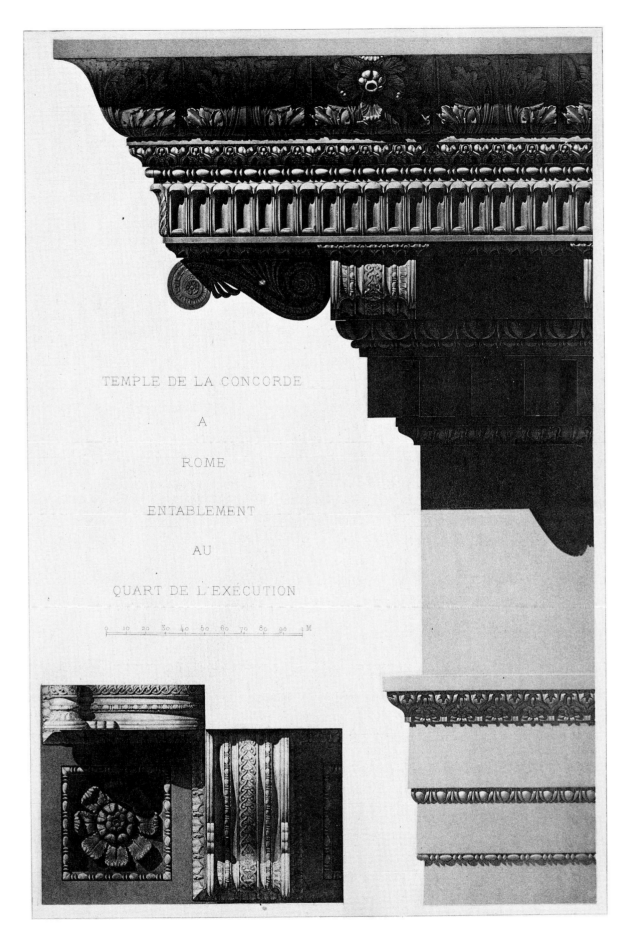

TEMPLE DE LA CONCORDE

A

ROME

ENTABLEMENT

AU

QUART DE L'EXECUTION

TEMPLE OF CONCORD IN ROME
Entablature, restored by Honoré Daumet

TEMPLE OF CONCORD IN ROME
Cornice Details, restored by Honoré Daumet

TEMPLE OF CONCORD IN ROME
Corinthian Capital and Base, restored by Honoré Daumet and the sculptor
Jean-Baptiste Carpeaux (1827–1875) *Grand Prix de Rome, 1854*

TEMPLE OF CASTOR AND POLLUX (Jupiter Stator) IN ROME
Column and Details, restored by Auguste Ancelet

TEMPLE
DE
JUPITER·STATOR

TEMPLE OF CASTOR AND POLLUX (Jupiter Stator) IN ROME
Cornice, restored by Auguste Ancelet

TEMPLE OF CASTOR AND POLLUX (Jupiter Stator) IN ROME
Soffit of Cornice and Bracket, restored by Auguste Ancelet

TEMPLE OF CASTOR AND POLLUX (Jupiter Stator) IN ROME
Corinthian Capital, restored by Auguste Ancelet

TEMPLE OF CASTOR AND POLLUX (Jupiter Stator) **IN ROME**
Section of Corinthian Capital, restored by Auguste Ancelet

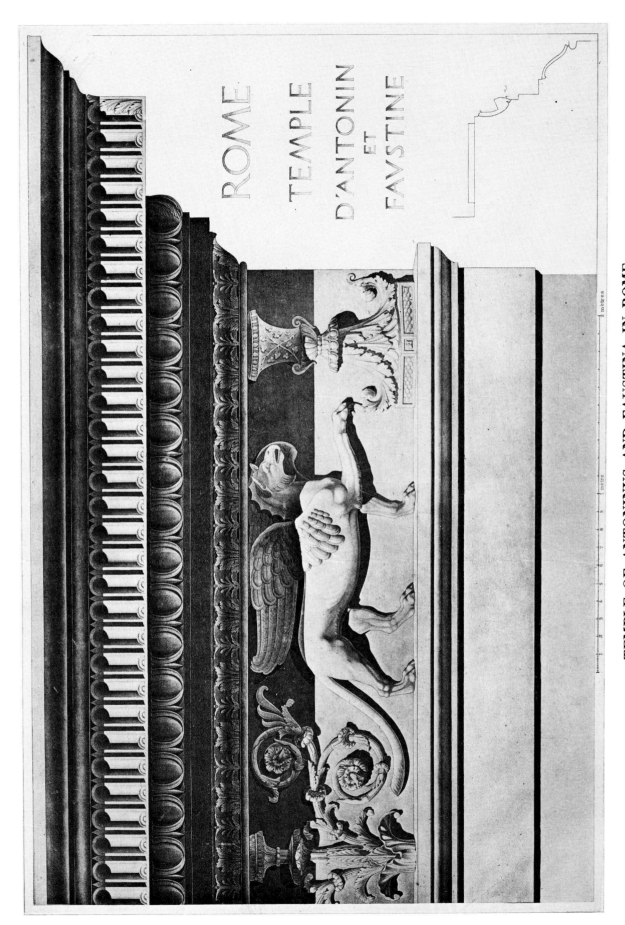

TEMPLE OF ANTONINUS AND FAUSTINA IN ROME
Entablature, restored by Alphonse-Alexandre Defrasse

81

ROME

TEMPLE DE VESPASIEN

P. BLONDEL

LEFUEL

TEMPLE OF VESPASIAN IN ROME
Entablature (see plate 40 for details of frieze), restored by Hector Lefuel
(1810–1881) *Grand Prix de Rome, 1839*; details by Paul Blondel

82

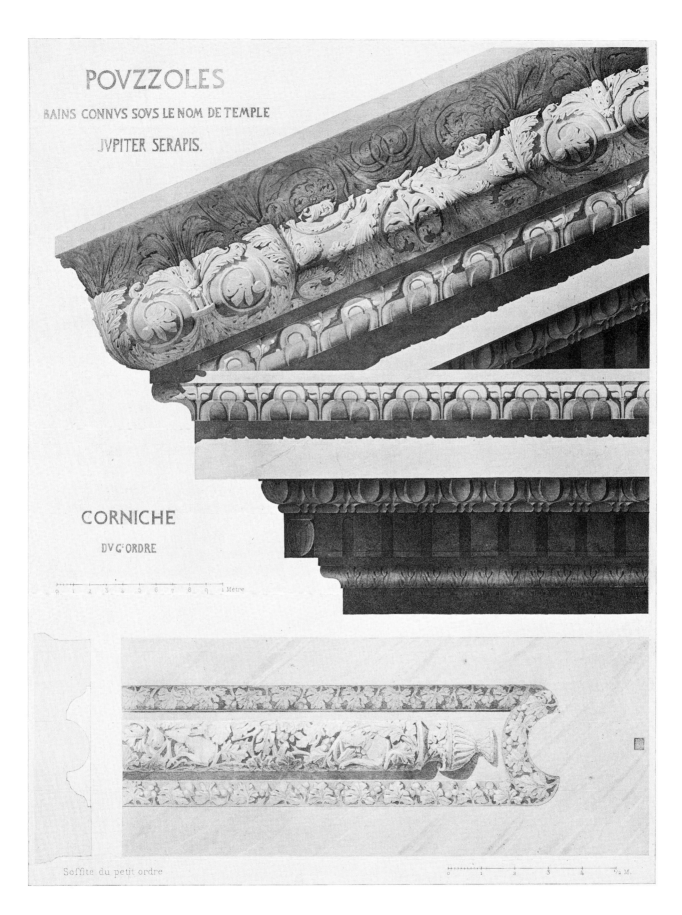

POVZZOLES

BAINS CONNVS SOVS LE NOM DE TEMPLE

JVPITER SERAPIS.

CORNICHE

DV G· ORDRE

1 Metre

Soffite du petit ordre

½ M.

TEMPLE OF SERAPIS AT POZZUOLI
Entablature, restored by Charles Garnier

ARCH OF TITUS
Arch and Details by Charles Girault

ARCHES OF SEPTIMIUS SEVERUS AND CONSTANTINE IN ROME

General View by Felix Duban (1797–1870) *Grand Prix de Rome, 1823*

Details, restored by Auguste Ancelet

85

ARCH OF SEPTIMIUS SEVERUS IN ROME
Details, restored by Auguste Ancelet

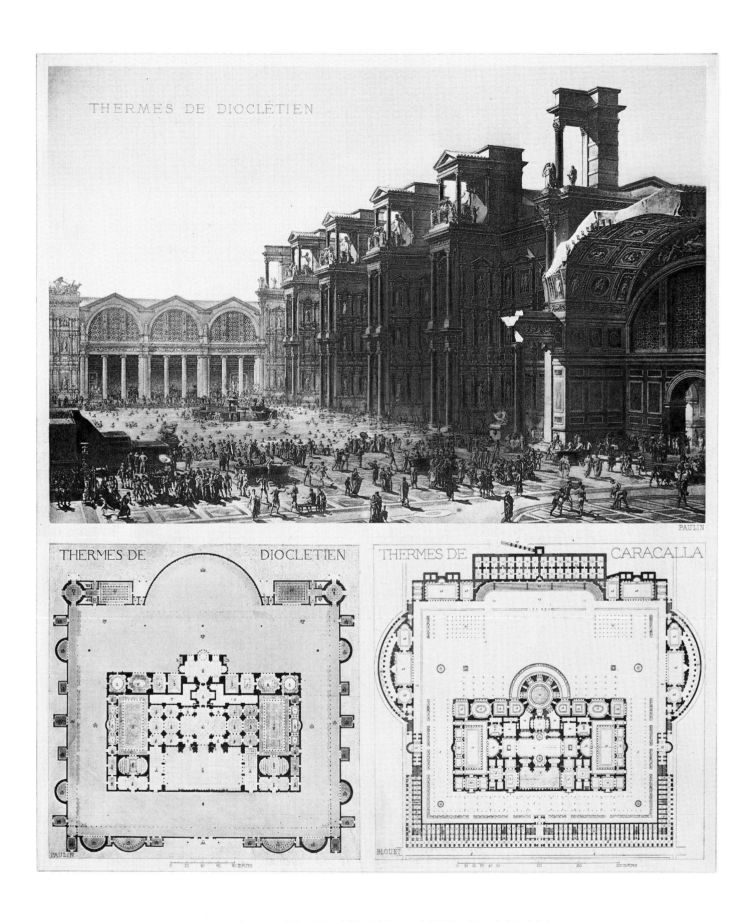

BATHS OF DIOCLETIAN AND BATHS OF CARACALLA
Restorations by Edmond Paulin and Abel Blouet (1795–1853)
Grand Prix de Rome, 1821

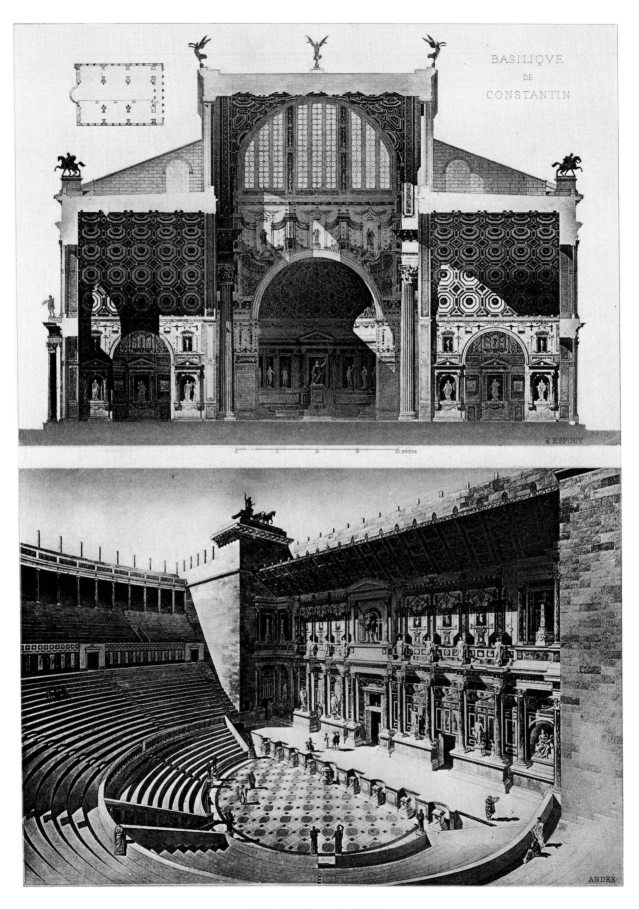

BASILIQVE
DE
CONSTANTIN

d'ESPOUY

ANDRÉ

THEATER AT OSTIA
Below, Restoration of interior by Pierre André

THE PARTHENON
Elevation, restored by Edouard Loviot

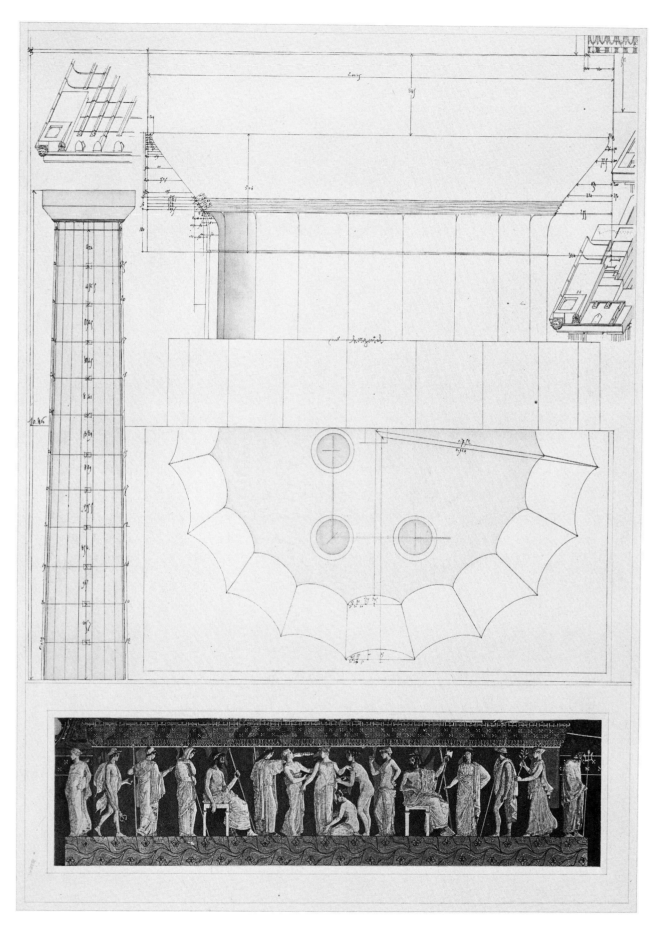

THE PARTHENON
Restoration by Edouard Loviot

SACRED PRECINCT OF DEMETER AT ELEUSIS
Elevation, restored by Victor Blavette

STATUE D'ESCULAPE

TEMPLE OF AESCULAPIUS AND SACRED PRECINCT AT EPIDAURUS
Restorations by Alphonse-Alexandre Defrasse

CHAPITEAU

DE

L'ORDRE

INTÉRIEUR

TEMPLE OF AESCULAPIUS AND SACRED PRECINCT AT EPIDAURUS
Corinthian Capital by Alphonse-Alexandre Defrasse

93

TOMB OF MAUSOLUS AT HALICARNASSUS

Elevation and Section by Louis Bernier. (Bernier's restoration, one of several, influenced
John Duncan in designing Grant's Tomb in New York City.)

TOMB OF MAUSOLUS AT HALICARNASSUS
Details restored by Louis Bernier

PROFIL

DE

L'ENTABLEMENT

DENTICULE

PARTIE INTÉRIEURE
DES CANNELURES

PROFIL
D'UNE AUTRE
FRISE DONT
IL NE RESTE
QU'UN
FRAGMENT

FRAGMENTS
DE LA
BASE
DE LA
COLONNE

DÉTAIL
D'UNE VOLUTE

COUPE
FAITE
A L'AXE
DU
COUSSINET

COUSSINET

COUPE

VERTICALE

COUPE HORIZONTALE

TOMB OF MAUSOLUS AT HALICARNASSUS
Details, restored by Louis Bernier

96

TOMB OF MAUSOLUS AT HALICARNASSUS
Details, restored by Louis Bernier

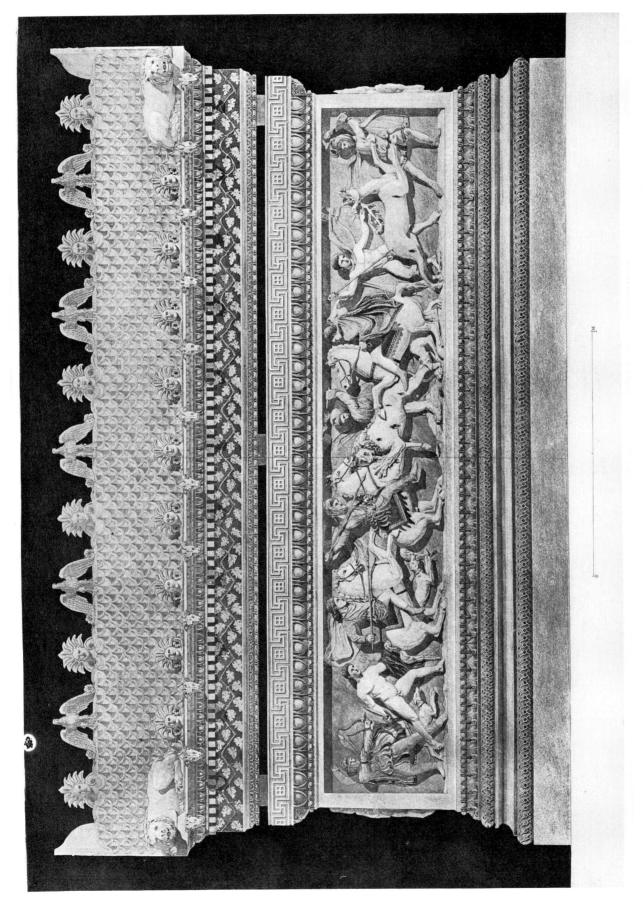

TOMB OF ALEXANDER FROM SIDON (NOW IN THE ISTANBUL MUSEUM)
Long Side by Ernest Hébrard (1875–?) Grand Prix de Rome, 1904

TOMB OF ALEXANDER FROM SIDON (NOW IN THE ISTANBUL MUSEUM)
Short Side by Ernest Hébrard

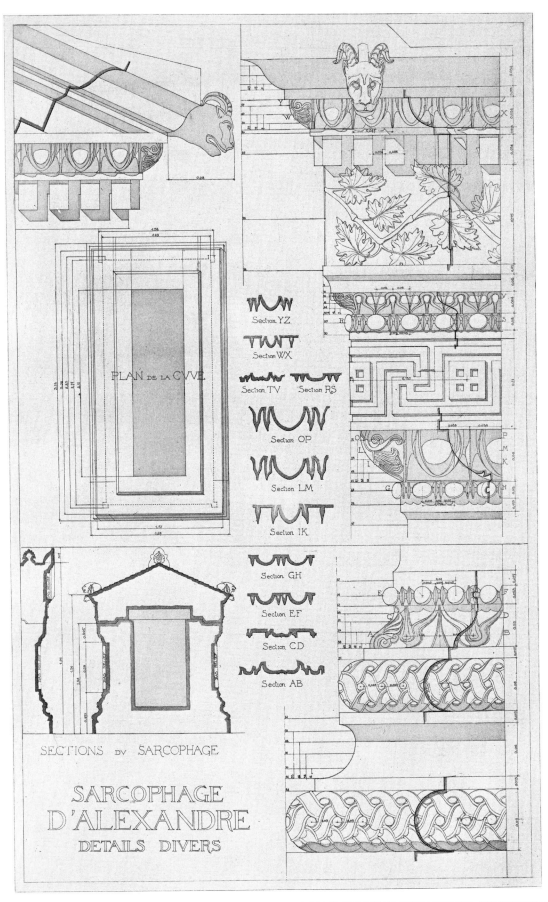

PLAN DE LA CUVE

Section YZ

Section WX

Section TV   Section RS

Section OP

Section LM

Section IK

Section GH

Section EF

Section CD

Section AB

SECTIONS DU SARCOPHAGE

SARCOPHAGE
D'ALEXANDRE
DETAILS DIVERS

TOMB OF ALEXANDER FROM SIDON (NOW IN THE ISTANBUL MUSEUM)
Plan, Section, and Details by Ernest Hébrard

TEMPLE

DE CASTOR ET POLLUX

TEMPLE OF CASTOR AND POLLUX IN CORA
Plan, Façade, and Capital by Théodore Labrouste (1799–1885)
Grand Prix de Rome, 1831

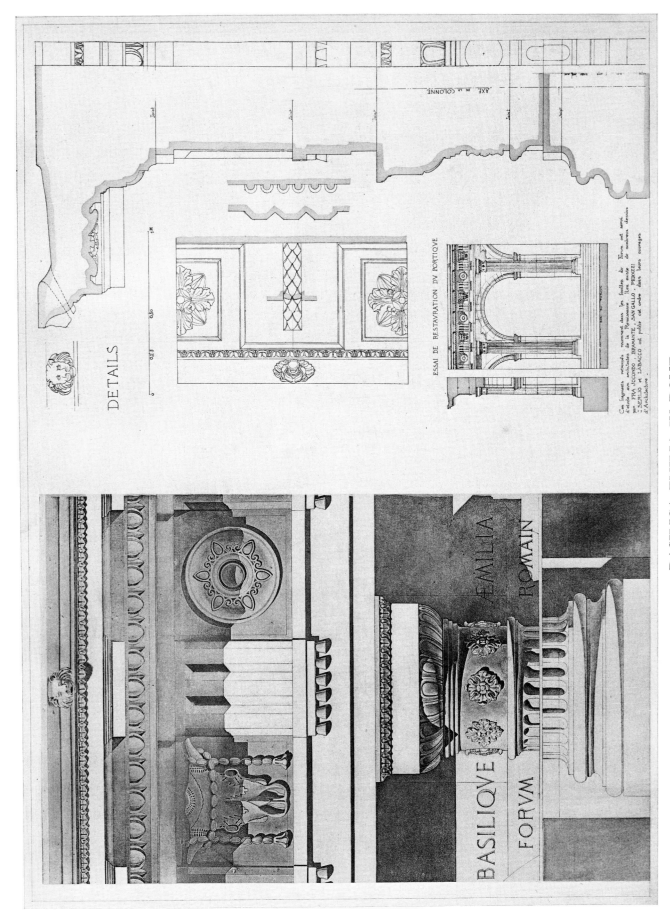

DETAILS

ESSAI DE RESTAVRATION DV PORTIQVE

AXE DE LA COLONNE

Ces fragments retrouvés, montrent dans les fouilles de Forum, ont servi d'études aux architectes de la Renaissance. Ils ont été dessiné de nombreux par FRA JOCONDO, BRAMANTE, SANGALLO, PERVZZI. SERLIO et LABACCO ont publié cet ordre dans leurs ouvrages d'Architecture.

ÆMILIA

ROMAIN

BASILIQVE

FORVM

BASILICA EMILIA IN ROME
Doric Order and Cornice, restored by Ernest Hébrard

102

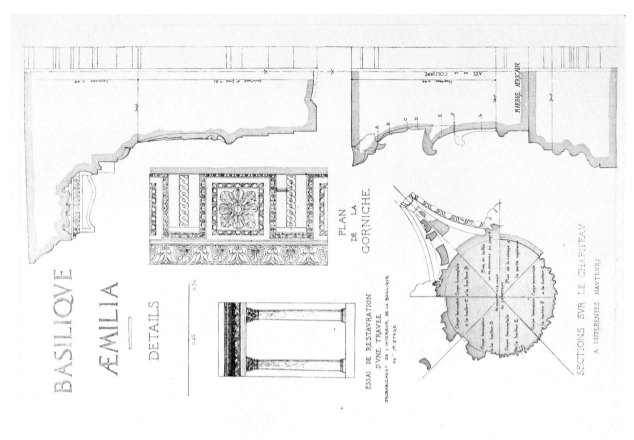

BASILICA EMILIA IN ROME
Corinthian Order and Cornice, restored by Ernest Hébrard

ARA PACIS AND BASILICA EMILIA IN ROME
Above, Detail of Ornament of the Ara Pacis, restored by Léon Jaussely (1875–?) *Grand Prix de Rome, 1903; below*, Ornamental Details of Frieze of the Basilica Emilia, restored by Ernest Hébrard

ROMAN FRAGMENTS
Various Motifs, Urns, Candelabra, etc., restored by Louis-Jean Hulot (1871–?)
Grand Prix de Rome, 1901

RESTAVRATION DV CHATEAV DE L'EAV IVLES.

PLAN   RESTAURÉ

FOUNTAIN OF AQUA JULIA IN ROME
Elevation and Plan, restored by Antoine-Martin Garnaud (1796–1861)
Grand Prix de Rome, 1817

CHATEAV·DE·L'EAV·ÍVLES·
FACADE·LATERALE·RESTAVREE

CHATEAV·DE·LEAV·ÍVLES
COVPE·RESTAVREE

IMP

PORTE DE TIBVR

FOUNTAIN OF AQUA JULIA IN ROME
Various details by Antoine-Martin Garnaud

TROPHIES OF MARIUS

Trophies as They Stand on the Capitoline by Antoine-Martin Garnaud

THE PANTHEON
Section of Interior by Achille Leclère (1785–1853)
Grand Prix de Rome, 1808

109

VOUTE
DV
VESTIBULE

VOUTE
DE LA ROTONDE

TÊTES DE CLOVS
DE LA
GRANDE PORTE

COLONNES
DE LA ROTONDE

THE PANTHEON
Details of Vault Coffering, Nail Heads of Door, Column by Achille Leclère
(see plates 58–65)

ARCH OF TITUS
Details by Auguste Guénepin (1780–1842) *Grand Prix de Rome, 1805*
(see plate 84)

111

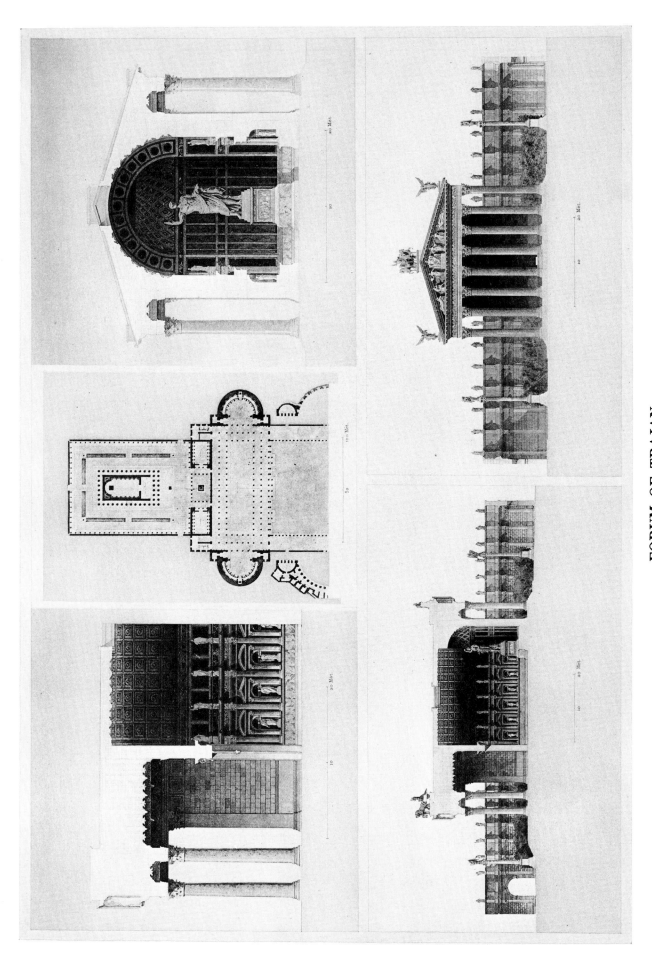

FORUM OF TRAJAN
Elevation, restored by Julien Gaudet

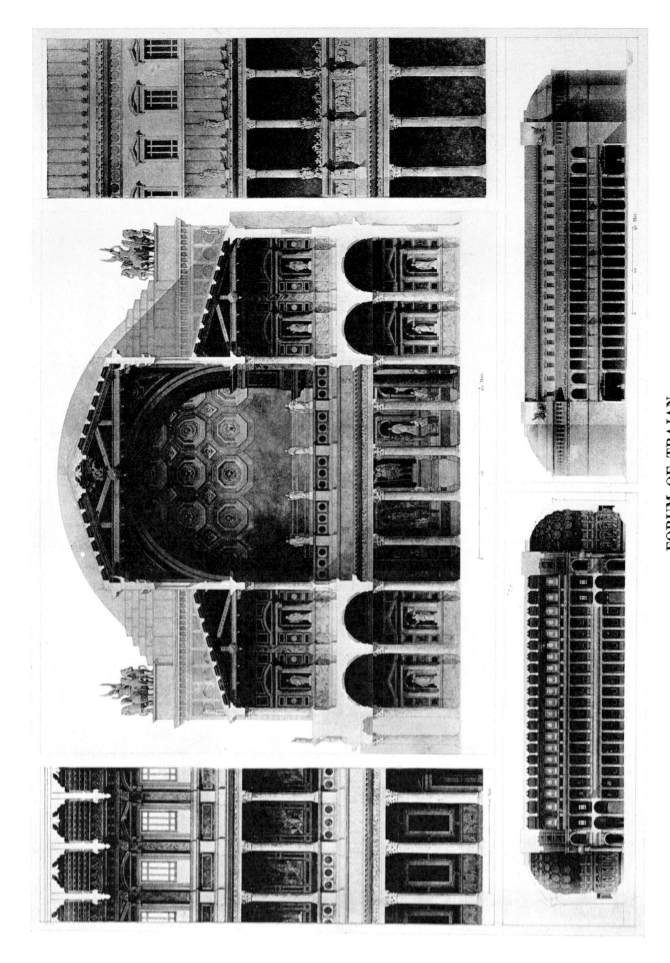

FORUM OF TRAJAN
Elevation, restored by Julien Gaudet

113

Plan du dessous de la Soffite

FORUM OF TRAJAN

Details of Entablature Found in the Forum, restored by Mathieu-Prosper Morey
(1805–1878) *Grand Prix de Rome, 1831*

IMP·CAESARI·DIVI·NERVAE·F·NERVAE
TRAIANO·OPTIMO·AVG·GERMANIC
DACICO·PONT·MAX·TR·POT·XVIIII·IMP·IX
COS·VI·P·P·PROVIDENTISSIMO·PRINCIPI
SENATVS·P·Q·R·QVOD·ACCESSVM
ITALIAE·HOC·ETIAM·ADDITO·EX·PECVNIA·SVA
PORTV·TVTIOREM·NAVIGANTIBVS·REDDIDERIT

PLOTINAE
AVG
CONIVG·AVG

DIVAE
MARCIANAE
AVG
SORORI·AVG

ARC DE TRAJAN A ANCONE

ARCH OF TRAJAN AT ANCONA

Elevation and Section by Théodore Labrouste

TEMPLE OF CASTOR AND POLLUX (Jupiter Stator) IN ROME
Elevation of Main Façade, Ceiling of Architrave and Shaft of Column by Tieleman
Franciscus Suys (1783–1861) *Grand Prix de Rome, 1812* (see plates 76–80)

116

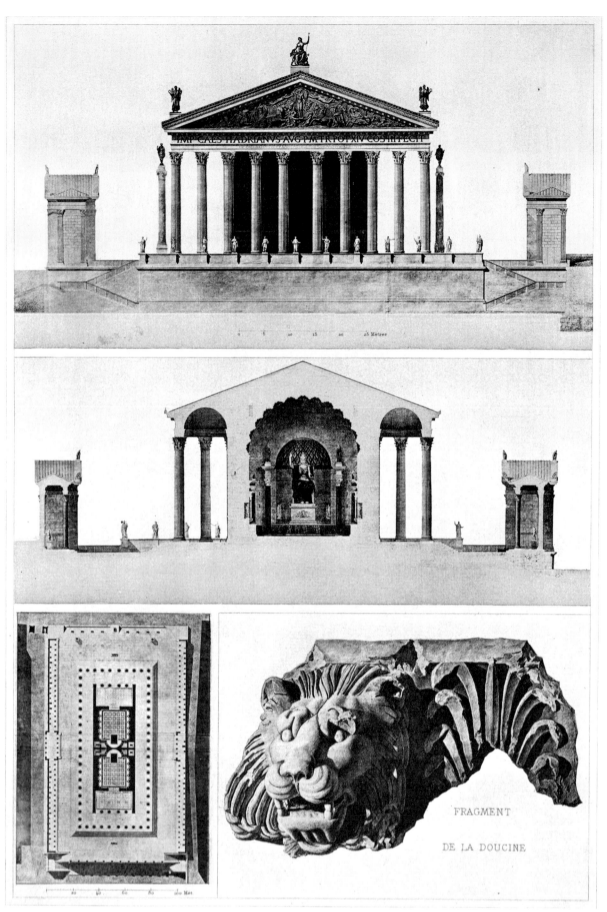

TEMPLE OF VENUS AND ROME IN ROME
Main Façade, Cross Section, Fragments of Cyma by Léon Vaudoyer
(1803–1872) *Grand Prix de Rome, 1826*

FRONTON   RESTAURÉ

IMP·CAES·HADRIANVS·AVG·P·M·TR·POT·XIV·COS·III·FECIT

IMP·CAES·MAXENTIVS·P·F·AVGVSTVS·INCENDIO·CONSVMPTVM·RESTITVIT

TEMPLE OF VENUS AND ROME IN ROME
Interior Details and Pediment by Léon Vaudoyer

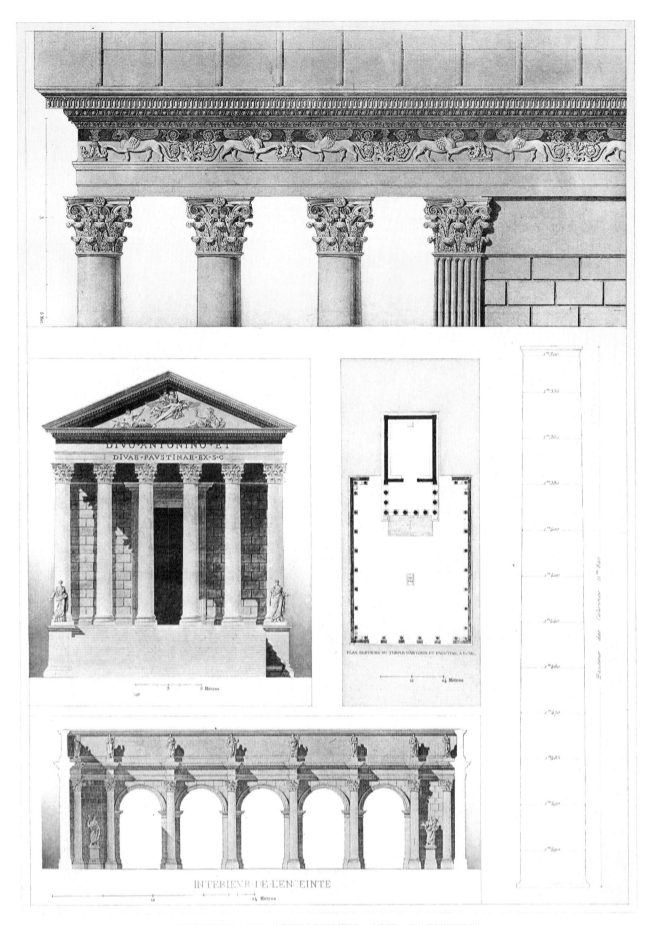

TEMPLE OF ANTONINUS AND FAUSTINA
Detail of Entablature, Main Façade, Plan, Elevation of Interior Court, Shaft of Column
by Jean-François-Julien Mesnager (1783–1864) *Grand Prix de Rome, 1800* (see plate 81)

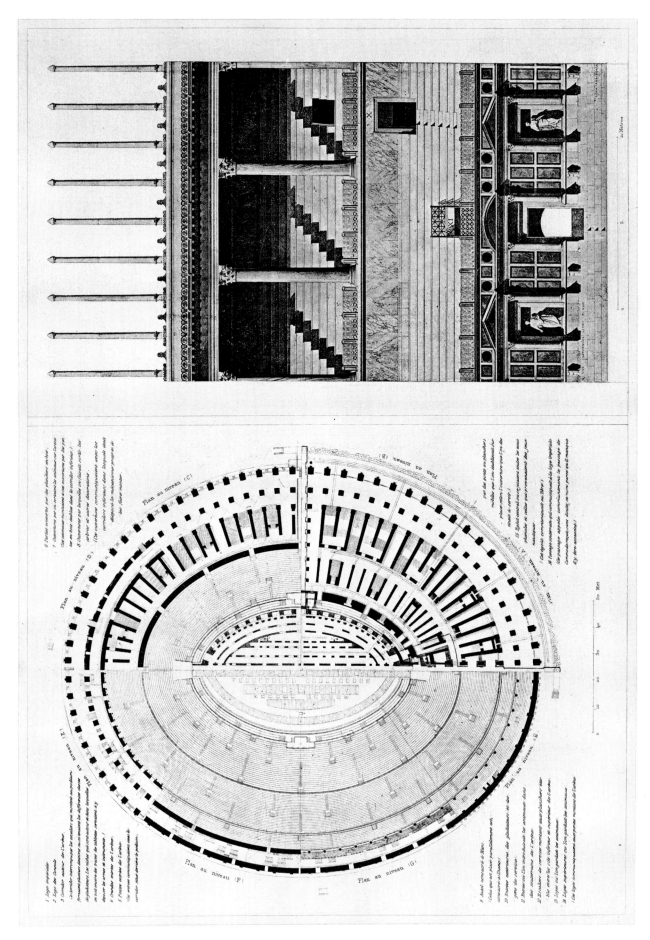

THE COLISEUM

Plan of Whole, Interior Elevations by Louis Duc

COUPE SUR LE GRAND AXE

FAÇADE SUR LE PETIT AXE

THE COLISEUM

Cross-Section along Main Axis and Façade of Short Axis by Louis Duc

THE COLISEUM
Detail of Façade by Louis Duc

ANCIENT CAPITAL IN SANTA MARIA IN TRASTEVERE
Main Side of Capital by Paul Bigot (1870–1942) Grand Prix de Rome, 1900

CHAPITEAV·ANTIQVE

AV·TIERS·DE·L'EXECVTION

PLAN
DV
CHAPITEAV·RENVERSE

1 Metre

FACE·LATERALE

SVR
L'
AXE

SVR
LA
VOLVTE

BIGOT

FRAGMENT·DE·L'ARA·PACIS

D·AVGVSTE·DETAIL·AVX·2/3·DE·L'EXECVTION

150 Cent^{mes}   JAUSSELY

ANCIENT CAPITAL IN SANTA MARIA IN TRASTEVERE. Lateral Side, Plan,
and Section of the Capital by Paul Bigot; ARA PACIS (NOW IN THE VILLA MEDICI), restored by Léon Jaussely

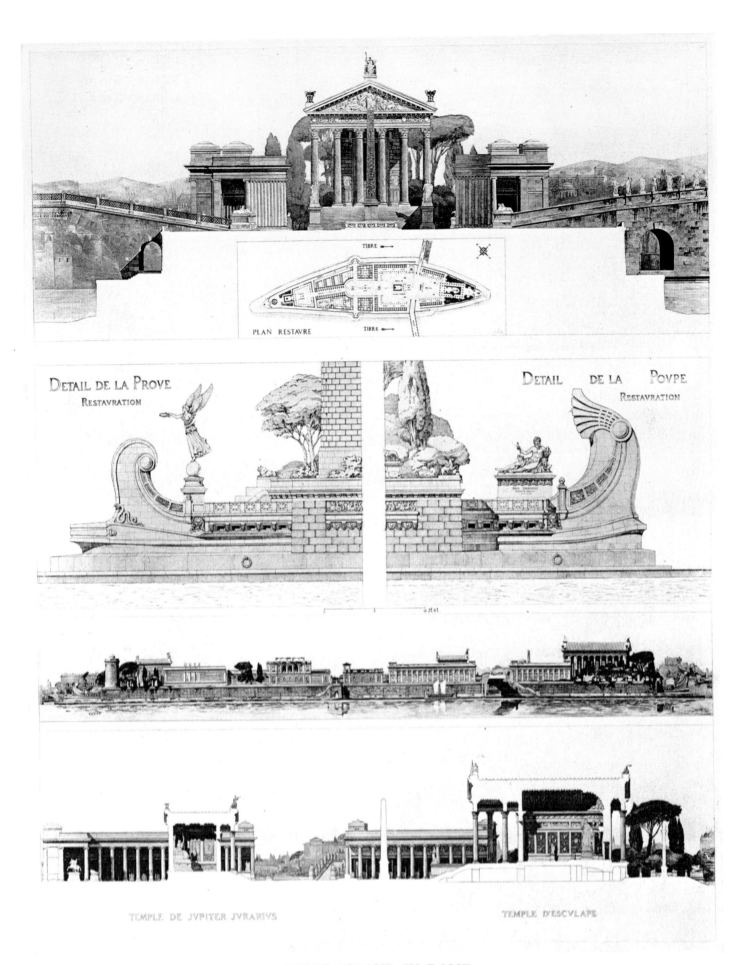

TIBER ISLAND IN ROME
Plan, Elevation, Section, and Details, restored by Auguste Patouillard
(1869–?) *Grand Prix de Rome, 1895*

Circue d'Adrien
Théâtre de Pompée et Portique
Théâtre Balbus

Stade de Domitien
(Cirque ogonal)

Mausolée d'Auguste
Thermes d'Agrippa
Temple et portique de Philippe

Pantheon

TIBER ISLAND IN ROME
Bird's-Eye View of the Island by Auguste Patouillard

BASILICA OF CONSTANTINE IN ROME
Cross Section and Details by Martin-Pierre Gauthier (1790–1855)
Grand Prix de Rome, 1810 and Hector d'Espouy

DU
TEMPLE·DE·LA·CONCORDE
A·ROME
CHAPITEAU · BASE
ET
FRAGMENTS
AU
TIERS
DE
L'EXECUTION

TO·THE·DEFENDERS·OF·THE·UNION·1861·1865